Capitalist Realism

Is There No Alternative?

T0350025

CollectiveInk

First published by Zero Books, 2014
Second edition published by Zero Books, 2022
Zero Books is an imprint of Collective Ink Ltd.,
Unit 11, Shepperton House, 89 Shepperton Road, London, N1 3DF
office@collectiveinkbooks.com
www.collectiveinkbooks.com
www.zero-books.net

For distributor details and how to order please visit the 'Ordering' section on our website.

Text copyright: Mark Fisher 2008

ISBN: 978 1 80341 430 0
978 1 80341 431 7 (ebook)

All rights reserved. Except for brief quotations in critical articles or reviews, no part of this book may be reproduced in any manner without prior written permission from the publishers.

The rights of Mark Fisher as author have been asserted in accordance with the Copyright, Designs and Patents Act 1988.

A CIP catalogue record for this book is available from the British Library.

Design: Lapiz Digital Services
Cover design by Rebecca Wright
charcoalstrudio.co.uk

UK: Printed and bound by CPI Group (UK) Ltd, Croydon, CR0 4YY
Printed in North America by CPI GPS partners

We operate a distinctive and ethical publishing philosophy in all areas of our business, from our global network of authors to production and worldwide distribution.

Capitalist Realism

Is There No Alternative?

Mark Fisher

zer0
books

London, UK
Washington, DC, USA

Mark Fisher's writing put Zer0 Books on the map in 2009. *Capitalist Realism* continues to define our mission. The world lost a radical thinker when Fisher left us in January of 2017. He was highly respected both as a music writer and a theorist and wrote regularly for frieze, New Statesman, Sight & Sound and The Wire, where he was acting deputy editor for a year. He was a Visiting Fellow at Goldsmiths, University Of London, and maintained one of the most successful weblogs on cultural theory, k-punk (http://k-punk.abstractdynamics.org).

Also by Mark Fisher:

Ghosts of My Life: Writings on Depression, Hauntology and Lost Futures
Paperback: 9781780992266
ebook: 9781782796244

The Resistible Demise of Michael Jackson
Paperback: 9781846943485
ebook: 9781789042702

To my wife, Zöe, my parents, Bob and Linda,
and the readers of my website

CONTENTS

Foreword
by Zoe Fisher

I vividly remember the months when Mark was finishing the last draft of *Capitalist Realism*. We had left London to live in Suffolk, a place that was special to him as it was full of happy memories from his childhood holidays. The breathing space our move gave him allowed Mark to devote proper, uninterrupted time to completing the book. Once in Suffolk, he told me that the ideas had come more easily and he was excited about completing the project. "I would be really pleased if it sold 500 copies", he told me one day when we were out walking in Woodbridge.

During that period, Mark was also busy trying to find lecturing work and build up his freelance writing — he did a brief stint working at *The Wire* as a temporary guest editor, but his main point of contact with his readers was still his blog. Those years were admittedly tough as Mark struggled to secure a permanent academic appointment, but they were also a happy and optimistic time for us. Mark enjoyed the contrast of his busy days in London with his time in Suffolk where there were fewer demands on him, allowing him to concentrate on other projects such as *On Vanishing Land*. By the time of the launch party for *Capitalist Realism*, arriving just days before we had found out I was pregnant with our son George, it felt like things were coming together, and I remember Mark having the best time that evening, surrounded by people who made him feel energised and inspired.

I know that the success of *Capitalist Realism* really took Mark by surprise, and what followed over the next few years was Mark being able to, as he put it, "live out his dream" — lecturing at Goldsmiths — but still having time to work on his writing and traveling to various guest lectures and speaking engagements.

In true Mark-style, even after our son George was born in 2010, he managed to continue to be all things to all people. He never wanted to turn down an invitation to speak somewhere or an offer to write, as these things never felt like work to him. To observe Mark lecturing or speaking at an event was to see him in his element, as exciting and fulfilling for him as the audiences he communicated with. Just as importantly, he told me that he did not have to look over his shoulder for his depression anymore, and even though I knew that those feelings of worthlessness and doubt would never magically disappear, I was relieved that they were no longer in the foreground, and I hoped they could be kept at bay. Mark was often moved by individuals who felt that they were able to share their own experiences of mental health with him, inspired by the fact that he had always been so candid and open about his own struggles, and the release of the book was a catalyst for others to speak up.

Since those days, the grief and pain of losing Mark never gets smaller, but George and I have had to learn how to build a new life around it — it is the hardest thing we will ever have to do. Mark remains George's reference point and is still strangely present in any decision or event that occurs in our family. George is beginning to consider his dad, not through the eyes of the six-year-old he was when Mark died, but through the eyes of the adolescent he is now. As George explores his emerging sense of self, I see Mark's influence as a huge part of who he is becoming. He is very much Mark's son; his mannerisms and expressions, his intellectual curiosity, his dedication, his insistence on having the last word in a contentious situation, his love for Marvel, football and living in Felixstowe. Over the last few years, George has begun to learn more about who Mark was in the wider world — to his friends, colleagues and followers. He will watch Mark's lectures on YouTube, look up his writing online and see what others thought of him.

I can't comprehend the power of seeing a stranger on the underground, or at an airport, reading a book that your dad has written, but what I do know is that it fills George with a sense of pride and a knowledge that his dad was someone who was significant to many people. George and I know that we are not the only ones who lost Mark, and are not the only ones left with a space that is impossible to fill.

I think back to that conversation in Woodbridge, about Mark's hopes that 500 copies of *Capitalist Realism* sold would feel like success to him, and I am in awe of how much he achieved and how many people he reached. The fact that his ideas are still relevant and discussed will not bring Mark back, but there is no need for them to. He will always be a part of our lives.

Introduction

by Alex Niven

'Dear Mark,' began an email of January 2010 to a man I had never met:

> I read your book *Capitalist Realism* last week, and it felt like coming up for air after a long time spent underwater. I would like to thank you from the bottom of my heart for giving such eloquent expression to pretty much everything that needed to be said, and for providing a reason to hope, when I for one was just about ready to despair.

Reading these phrases back now, well over a decade later, I'm slightly embarrassed by the wording, but not at all by the sentiment. At the time, I had just suffered a head-on collision with the music industry, after a long period of post-teen crisis sparked by a series of family bereavements. I was depressed, I suppose — in the trough of my mid-twenties, and looking for explanations about why even the basics of twenty-first-century work, social, and private life seemed so hard, so disempowered, so existentially thankless.

For me — and for many others in a similar place both then and since — encountering *Capitalist Realism* really did feel like *surfacing* (to cite the title and central theme of Margaret Atwood's haunting novel of 1972 — a canonical text for Mark). In a society where everything was set up to make you think that your emotional wellbeing began and ended with your own personal psychodrama, perhaps the simplest, most important thing Mark's book did was to suggest that, just maybe, mental suffering might have something to do with structural flaws in society as a whole. Put another way, in the thick of a political system which endlessly promoted the notion that we were all ultimately alone, *Capitalist Realism* announced that we were all suffering together — and also, more hopefully, that if we were to realise this, and somehow make connections between our several hardships, we would be taking the first step towards doing something we seemed to have mostly forgotten about by the late Noughties: mounting an organised resistance.

Before anything else, this is the vital, near-spiritual message which came along with the short, sharp, explosive text that was *Capitalist Realism*, published in the last weeks of 2009 on the eve of a new and tumultuous decade. At its most basic level, whatever political and theoretical nuances it might otherwise have implied, this was a book which called for a joining of human hands.

This is partly why, despite my timidity, and despite the fact that I didn't usually do this sort of thing, I worked up the courage to send its author a short thank-you note in the first days of 2010 — and received a short, encouraging response from him the following day (Mark was famously generous with time and support when it came to helping younger writers — sometimes, it must be said, to the detriment of his own workload and wellbeing). It is also why *Capitalist Realism* went on to become one of the seminal political texts of the 2010s, and indeed the whole of the twenty-first century thus far. Unlike most forms of writing, in all genres, this was a book which set aside solipsism, irony, and ego to imagine a community of people united by a simple belief that the way things were was not okay — and then to dangle the tantalising possibility that this imagined community might soon become a social reality capable of changing the world. As one of the most evocative chapter titles in *Capitalist Realism* demanded, with almost childlike clarity and hopefulness: *What if you held a protest and everyone came?*

But in spite of such lyric universalism, *Capitalist Realism* was also the product of a set of specific, even bathetic local circumstances — many of which have been forgotten or passed over in the years since this peculiar essay became one of the primary texts of the modern era.

The first of these is the distinctive personal journey which led to its publication. Although, somewhat incredibly, *Capitalist Realism* was Mark Fisher's first proper book, it marked the end of two decades of non-conformist intellectual questing for its author. In fact, given that Mark was 41 when it was published — a fair bit older than the average age for a first-time author — it should probably be viewed as a belated breakthrough at the end of an unusually long professional apprenticeship. And yet it was no immature *Bildungsroman*. In the years prior to his first authored book, Mark had made strenuous attempts to make the case that there might be a viable alternative to the received, late-twentieth-century template for writing, scholarship, and thinking. *Capitalist Realism* was merely the final proof that he was right.

After a working-class upbringing in the English East Midlands, Mark benefited in his formative years from contact with the fertile intellectual climate of British higher education in the late Eighties and early Nineties (crucially, a time before the introduction of tuition fees in 1998 triggered the radical marketisation of the British state system). As a postgraduate student at the University of Warwick for much of the Nineties, he was one of the key members of the Cybernetic Culture Research Unit (CCRU), an 'accelerationist' tendency dedicated to imagining new cultural modes on the far side of late-capitalist dystopias. Though this is not the place to provide a detailed summary of the CCRU and its often occult subculture, I think we can say that Mark's training in this aberrant faction hardwired him to avoid following a traditional career path in the years after he completed his PhD, on 'cybernetic theory-fiction', at Warwick in 1999.

Further aided (and impeded in equal measure) by the fickleness of twenty-first-century academia, Mark would make good on his cybernetic training to become one of the first truly indispensable presences on the still-young internet in the early-to-mid Noughties. Free from the strictures of a secure academic job, Mark made a virtue of what would later be called 'precarity' by occupying the centre of a scene described by Simon Reynolds as a 'constellation of blogs'. For a five-year period lasting roughly from the Iraq War to the Global Financial Crisis, this cabal of theoretical and pop-cultural discussion was home to some of the best, most entertaining writing anywhere on the planet. Circa 2006, chancing on some of the sites in this corner of the so-called blogosphere — weird avatars for their IRL authors with aliases like *Kino Fist, The Impostume, blissblog,* and *Sit Down Man, You're a Bloody Tragedy* — you would tend to encounter long, usually pretty good natured debates, which were begun in the posts themselves and then endlessly elaborated in their byzantine comment sections. Subjects included — but were not limited to — the legacy of M. R. James's ghost stories, the misuses of Derridean theory, the legacy of post-war state-funded broadcasting, Wu Tang Clan, *V for Vendetta,* the pointlessness of mainstream media, and the imaginative paucity of Arctic Monkeys lyrics.

In the middle of this informal grouping, and supplying most of its ideational energy, was Mark's seminal *k-punk* blog. As well as acting as a hub for the wider scene's primitive version of social media, *k-punk* was also the space where Mark developed a philosophically expansive body of work, which used a series of mainly cultural examples to try to find an escape route from the airless atmosphere of the High Noughties — surely the tackiest, most desultory interlude in modern history.

When the Global Financial Crisis descended to smash apart the complacency of this micro-period in 2008, Zer0 Books emerged — a lightning response to a putative 'revolutionary moment', as well as the culmination of years of creative brainstorming on the blogosphere. Set up by Mark and a pair of (non-CCRU) Warwick pals — the novelist Tariq Goddard and the academic Matteo Mandarini (with publicist Emma Goddard completing the lineup) — the foundation of Zer0 marked the point at which this hitherto marginal tendency — perhaps the only really authentic literary avant-garde in Britain at the time — started to make serious inroads into the mainstream of reading and reviewing. Though *Capitalist Realism* was not the first Zer0 book (it was preceded in 2009 by texts such as Owen Hatherley's architecture polemic *Militant Modernism* — and indeed by Mark's own edited collection, *The Resistible Demise of Michael Jackson*), it was clearly a manifesto of sorts for the new publishing imprint — a book-length expansion of the actual manifesto Mark wrote for the inside cover of every Zer0 book, which railed against "cretinous anti-intellectualism" and "expensively educated hacks", and called for an "idea of publishing as a making public of the intellectual".

Over time, *Capitalist Realism* would sell well over 100,000 copies in its English-language version alone, to become something like the *Unknown Pleasures* of the Zer0 narrative. Indeed, in ways that would later become tragically apposite, Zer0 was in a deep sense a sort of latter-day attempt to repeat the example of post-punk indie label Factory Records — with the grey, featureless landscape of twenty-first-century publishing standing in for the Seventies backdrop which lay behind Joy Division's seminal modernist noir. As in the case of *Unknown Pleasures* and Factory, *Capitalist Realism* and Zer0 would ultimately engender a sort of filmic saga which underlined just how objectively intriguing — and how subjectively painful — it is when anti-capitalists try to turn the structures of the market in on itself in a sustained and vigorous way. But that is a story for another time and place.

So much for the publishing narrative of *Capitalist Realism* — a sort of making flesh of the internet's virtual energies by a maverick faction intent on reviving the best aspects of the late-twentieth-century counterculture. But what of the wider historical backdrop against which the book positions itself as both corrective and critique?

As we have seen, *Capitalist Realism* was on one level a product of the specific environment of Noughties Britain. With hindsight, from the vantage point of our own era of creeping authoritarianism and looming ecological catastrophe, we might be tempted to look kindly on this period of relative social stability and comparatively high living standards. But we should be clear that it represented a particular kind of dystopia for Mark and for many other members of the Zer0 circle. Away from more complex debates about the deepening inequality which occurred under Third Way liberalism (of which more momentarily), it is important to grasp that much of the sense of desperation Mark harnessed in *Capitalist Realism* arose from a historically distinct *feeling* at this time that there was no visible opposition — anywhere, whatsoever — to a slowly worsening status quo.

After a flare-up of anti-capitalist protest in the very early part of the decade (the heyday of Naomi Klein's anti-globalisation screed *No Logo*), there was a drastic settling-down in much of the world in the mid-to late-Noughties. At some unspecified point during these years, a mood of depressive apathy came to predominate above all else. The sense that *there was no alternative* to globalised capitalism, to cite the central refrain of *Capitalist Realism*, had of course been pervasive since at least as far back as the early Nineties, when the end of Actually Existing Socialism in Eastern Europe signalled the start of neoliberalism's imperial phase. But it was only really in the years immediately preceding the Global Financial Crisis that this apparently realistic — actually fatalistic — world-spirit became truly hegemonic.

In the context of Britain, broadly representative of developed countries throughout the world, the sense of hopeless entropy had been encouraged by the political misdeeds of the presiding New Labour government. After coming to power on a wave of optimism (even among many radicals) in 1997, this centrist or centre-right administration had spent its first term in government (1997–2001) triangulating between neoconservatism (tough talk on immigration and benefits claimants, continued privatisation of public amenities, fawning support for big business) and some genuinely radical reforms, most notably in foreign policy (such as the referendums for Scottish and Welsh devolution in 1997 and the Good Friday Agreement for peace in the north of Ireland in 1998). However, by 2003 at the latest, when the Blair government's foreign brief took a sharp turn to the right with the onset of the Iraq War, New Labour had become a far more typical neoliberal proposition in the classic Reaganite-Thatcherite mould.

As privatisation reforms in the National Health Service continued apace, and as the Blair regime raised (and threatened to further raise) the university tuition fees they had first introduced in 1998, there was a strong sense of decline and fall in British culture — especially among younger people — which was nonetheless offset and obscured by a housing-market bubble and a seemingly robust economy which guaranteed a decent standard of living for many older professionals (though not, as we will see, those in the increasingly besieged public sector). The mass-media expression of this zeitgeist was a glut of ultra-derivative, weirdly hyped guitar bands like Kaiser Chiefs, Razorlight and the Zutons, and a venal celebrity culture epitomised by exploitative TV shows like *Big Brother* and *I'm a Celebrity ... Get Me Out of Here!* (not to mention, at the bottom of the barrel, trashy twilight-of-print magazines like *Heat*, *Nuts* and *Zoo*). For the most part, in the years after the largest protest in human history (the February 2003 anti-Iraq War demonstration) was roundly ignored by Blair and his ilk, it felt as though we were trapped inside an endlessly reloading cycle of late-capitalist tawdriness, with no counterculture or coalition of dissent to offer even a modicum of friction, let alone relief.

It was into this suffocating historical moment that *Capitalist Realism* dropped like a bomb in the run-up to Christmas 2009, after a bewildering year or so in which a tottering political system had been subject to a series of ineffectual patch-up jobs (the bailout of the banking system after the financial crisis, the election of neoliberal-lite US president Barack Obama, half-hearted attempts to "clean up" British politics after a protracted scandal about exorbitant MP expense claims, and so on and so forth *ad nauseam*).

At a little under 25,000 words, Mark's book was clearly no expansive work of theory or wide-ranging political survey (though it was also something more than a really succinct manifesto like that of Marx and Engels, which is half the length). Nonetheless, there were certain fundamental keynotes struck in *Capitalist Realism*, which distinguished it from books in the same broad literary category — notably those of Fredric Jameson and Slavoj Žižek, Mark's immediate contemporary influences — and which ultimately gave it a purchase way beyond the more discursive work of his peers. As I suggested in talking about my own discovery of *Capitalist Realism*, there was a basic sense of righteousness and timeliness in the communitarian call to arms in Mark's text, which to an extent bypassed its more specific examples and gave it a charge of emotional revelation. Nonetheless, those real-world examples were in another sense fundamental to the core message Mark was trying to get across in the book, and they helped to ensure that this was no abstract theoretical prose-poem about the coming community.

At heart, the quotidian narrative of the book revolves around interconnected themes of the relationship between old and young, blocked generational handover, and the central role played by education and its professional structures in immiserating both teachers and students — and by extension, the civic and intellectual livelihood of society as a whole. Some years before debates about 'millennials' and 'zoomers' gained wide traction, Mark found an evocative metaphor for the newly vast generation gap of the twenty-first century in the plot of Alfonso Cuarón's 2006 film, *Children of Men* — the summary of which supplies *Capitalist Realism* with its eerily arresting opening. In Cuarón's dystopian near-future Britain (first imagined in the source text by the novelist-turned-Tory peer P. D. James), an entire society has mysteriously lost the ability to bear children. For Mark, this narrative demands to be read figuratively, as a basis for interrogating late-capitalism's presiding mood of stasis and fatalism. Moving from the pithy hook borrowed from Žižek and Jameson — that it is easier to imagine the end of the world than the end of capitalism (as embodied in the apocalyptic backdrop to Cuarón's film) — we are then presented with a dyad of more pointed provocations: "How long can a culture persist without the new?" and "What happens if the young are no longer capable of producing surprises?"

Once again, it's useful to stress that this emphasis on cultural stagnation was partly a response to the specific atmosphere of the later Noughties (nowadays, after the series of socio-political shocks which harried the Long 2010s, we would be much less likely to talk of a world devoid of 'surprises'). And yet the basic diagnosis of creative dearth has remained broadly accurate as a judgment on our wider historical epoch. In its outline, this theory is both an extension of the earlier Jamesonian critique of 'postmodernism' (as indeed Mark acknowledged), and a premonition of the discussions of 'retromania' (the idea that pop culture underwent a headlong retreat into its own past after the late Eighties) which would later climax with the publication of Simon Reynolds's 2011 study of that name — and, indeed, Mark's own 2014 anthology, *Ghosts of My Life* (this was very much a meme that had been nurtured and elaborated on the Noughties blog scene, of which both authors were key members).

But it was given a more solid grounding in *Capitalist Realism*, through a series of vignettes drawn from Mark's experiences of precarious academia. Embedded in one of the first really widely read critiques of late-capitalist public-sector work life, Mark's brilliant neologism 'market Stalinism' summed up what was actually going on in countless dismal offices and meeting rooms throughout the world at the time. In the typical public-sector workplace, Mark argued,

> what we have is not a direct comparison of workers' performance or output, but a comparison between the audited representation of that performance and output. Inevitably, a short-circuiting occurs, and work becomes geared towards the generation and massaging of representations rather than to the official goals of the work itself. Indeed, an anthropological study of local government in Britain argues that "More effort goes into ensuring that a local authority's services are represented correctly than goes into actually improving those services". This reversal of priorities is one of the hallmarks of a system which can be characterized without hyperbole as 'market Stalinism'. What late capitalism repeats from Stalinism is just this valuing of symbols of achievement over actual achievement.

This bold naming of the capitalist 'big Other' was of a piece — as Mark's adjacent allusion to Khrushchev's Stalin-denouncing 'Secret Speech' of 1956 makes plain — to a wider strategy in *Capitalist Realism*, which is evident from the title downwards. This was quite simply and brilliantly to foreground a broad comparison between late capitalism and the system it was supposed to have supplanted: the Actually Existing Socialism of the post-war Communist Eastern Bloc. But again, and indeed in another *détournement* of the Western stereotype that late-twentieth-century Eastern Europe was a place of cultural impoverishment, the portrayal of a civic landscape devoid of creative energy was part of a much wider argument: that neoliberal societies such as Britain and the United States were simply not *growing* by this stage of capitalist (un)development.

If elder academics and intellectuals were mentally boxed in and prevented from imagining new ways of being and doing, then, as Mark also suggested, the feeling of Kafkaesque helplessness and hopelessness in the face of the market-Stalinist bureaucracy was also filtering down into the minds of the young in their crucial formative years. Drawing on his own experiences of teaching in further education, Mark presented another ground-breaking diagnosis of an adolescent malaise he termed 'depressive anhedonia'. This he defined in the following terms, as one

> constituted not by an inability to get pleasure so much as ... by an inability to do anything else except pursue pleasure. There is a sense that 'something is missing' — but no appreciation that this mysterious, missing enjoyment can only be accessed beyond the pleasure principle. In large part this is a consequence of students' ambiguous structural position, stranded between their old role as subjects of disciplinary institutions and their new status as consumers of services ... Students are aware that if they don't attend for weeks on end, and/or if they don't produce any work, they will not face any meaningful sanction. They typically respond to this freedom not by pursuing projects but by falling into hedonic (or anhedonic) lassitude: the soft narcosis, the comfort food oblivion of Playstation, all-night TV and marijuana.

Predating the hegemony of the smartphone by some years, this analysis got right to the heart of why twenty-first-century youth culture had ground to a halt, in spite or perhaps because of the seeming liberality of postmodern capitalist societies. In a historical period where the suppression of personal freedom and fulfilment (as apparently embodied in the fallen communist regimes of the late-twentieth century) was seen as the ultimate evil, why did young people feel so unfulfilled and so lacking in vitality?

Going beyond stock — and by this point seriously outdated — doctrinaire Marxist talk of 'false consciousness', Mark presented a simple, empirically grounded, and utterly plausible explanation. Underneath the positivity and surface euphoria of the golden age of globalisation — which still just about lingered into the Late Noughties — *Capitalist Realism* demonstrated how the supremacy of the market had in fact led to the total subjection of citizens remodelled as consumers. Having been denied even a vocabulary of oppression by neoliberalism in the years of its ascendancy, there was radical power in Mark's ability to put a name to the forms of social control which many people felt but few could vocalise. This was, if you like, Khrushchev's Secret Speech remodelled for the years of reality TV, tuition fees, and the iPod Nano.

If some of the writing in *Capitalist Realism* feels just a tad dated today, it is partly because of the book's astonishing success in the years since its publication. Despite its substantial impact when it was first released in late 2009, the really viral spread of Mark's text occurred slightly later, beginning with the series of events which occurred in and around 2011 — the 'year of dreaming dangerously' in some accounts.

In a British context, the ground was laid for *Capitalist Realism*'s journey towards ubiquity by the student protests of late 2010 — which followed from the election of a right-wing Conservative-Liberal Democrat coalition government and its fateful decision to raise university tuition fees from around £3,000 per year to around £9,000 (in line, it should be pointed out, with a recommendation in a report commissioned by the outgoing New Labour Prime Minister Gordon Brown). This was, in a sense, the moment when all the discussion in *Capitalist Realism* of a dystopian education system heading for disaster began to seem truly prescient. As the prospect of massively enlarged student debt combined with the first onslaught of the Coalition government's 'austerity' programme (which saw savage, neoliberalism-*in-extremis* cuts right across the public sector), there was a feeling that a tipping point had finally been reached.

While Mark had juxtaposed his diagnoses of market Stalinism and depressive anhedonia with rallying criticisms that modern students seemed 'politically disengaged' and 'resigned to their fate', the protests which erupted throughout British cities against the tuition-fee rise suggested that such provocations might have been at least partly successful. Indeed, as vast crowds of student protestors were alternately kettled by police on London streets and abruptly radicalised by sit-ins and occupations in university buildings across Britain, it was clear that *Capitalist Realism* had itself played a key role in achieving what Mark characterised as 'a way out of the motivation/de-motivation binary'. In a blogpost written at the time, Mark celebrated the class composition of the student protests in London, commenting how

> (we) Lacan-reading hipsters were also there, *alongside* the *'banlieue*-style youth from Croydon, Peckham, the council estates of Islington.' In other words, this brought together working-class culture and Bohemia in something like the same way that art schools — so crucial to UK pop-art culture since the Fifties — used to.

That parenthetic 'we' was a characteristic gesture of modesty on Mark's part. In fact, the demonstrators in late 2010 were far more likely to be reading his own pragmatic reworkings of Lacanian theory in *Capitalist Realism* than anything written by

Lacan himself. As word of mouth about this almost uncannily timely book spread, and as the British protests led quickly into the far more momentous global irruptions of the Year of Dreaming Dangerously proper (the Arab Spring, Occupy Wall Street, the Spanish *Indignados* movement, the anti-austerity protests in Athens), it became more and more apparent that *Capitalist Realism* was one of the manifestos of choice for those involved in the radical outbursts of the early 2010s. As Mark had written in his stirring peroration to the book:

> The tiniest event can tear a hole in the grey curtain of reaction which has marked the horizons of possibility under capitalist realism. From a situation in which nothing can happen, suddenly anything is possible again.

Whereas such rhetoric had seemed like mere hopeful (perhaps wishful) thinking in the late Noughties, the events of 2010–2012 ensured that it was now something like straightforward reportage. As a new mood of militancy descended to replace the apathetic torpor of the previous decade, the strange, breathless mixture of present-tense grammar forms in this utopic rallying cry began to make a powerful kind of sense. Suddenly, it really did seem as though anything might be possible again.

What happened next is probably broadly familiar to most people — and now we begin to intrude onto our own ambiguous, still-unfolding present tense. Though the aftereffects of the radical breakthrough of the early 2010s rumbled on for the next decade or so, and though many leading figures on the contemporary left still credit this interlude (and its key text *Capitalist Realism*) as a conversion moment, it must be said that at the time of writing, much of the world seems to have fallen back into a state of paralysis not unlike that which provoked Mark's polemical anger back in the late Noughties.

In the Anglosphere, the channelling of radical energies into left-populist figures like Bernie Sanders and Jeremy Corbyn briefly dangled the possibility of large-scale political reform. But by the beginning of the 2020s, at the latest, both had been defeated with varying degrees of finality. Meanwhile, Syriza's experiment in leftist government in Greece fizzled out long ago, and the global Occupy movement has largely become a historical curiosity. Underneath it all, the structural weaknesses of global capitalism have continued to generate recurrent crises. But capitalist governments have somehow managed to hobble on in the absence of any really cogent alternative. With ecological catastrophe now even more of a clear and present danger than it was when *Capitalist Realism* was written, Mark's borrowed axiom about the end of the world being easier to imagine than the end of capitalism is, if anything, even more apposite.

Perhaps demographic change will eventually lead to a great reformist breakthrough, as radically inclined millennials and zoomers come to dominate global governments in the approach to the 2030s. But we have to face the fact that while leftist ideas and attitudes are far more influential and more frequently articulated now than they were in the late Noughties, the call for a revival of protest and activism by what might be termed the *Capitalist Realism* generation has not yet generated any really lasting radical outcomes (let alone sparked anything like the political revolutions of the past). At the same time, fascism and the far-right are resurgent, raising the possibility of a capitalist collapse that will lead to the triumph of militarism and authoritarianism rather than any more humane egalitarian overhaul.

The personal postscript to *Capitalist Realism* was, of course, also one of sadness and broken dreams. While the book brought Mark acclaim and a wide readership, it did not bring him the lasting professional success it merited — and regardless of its (lack of) impact on his career, the attention the book garnered in the first half of the 2010s had little effect either way on his declining mental health. It is important to make clear that Mark's tragic suicide in January 2017 had nothing directly to do with *Capitalist Realism*. Nothing would be so crass — and totally unfounded — as to say that Mark's decision to take his own life was due to disappointment that the revival of protest he had prophesied and provoked in 2009 had appeared to run aground by early 2017 — or to draw glib analogies between his personal struggles and the socio-historical narrative of the 2010s. Nonetheless, I think we can at least say that Mark's death was indeed an event with wider social impact — mostly because it deprived us of an unusually eloquent and perceptive social commentator, and because it ruled out the possibility that there would ever be a proper sequel to the astonishing generational manifesto that was *Capitalist Realism*.

And yet, when all is said and done, and setting aside all questions of historical relevance, we have ultimately to heed the central argument of Mark's masterpiece — which is at least as profound as anything in the philosophy of Kierkegaard, Hegel or Marx. At bottom, *Capitalist Realism* tells us that when a community or an individual is being oppressed, there really is no more radical or necessary act than to look beyond the apparent limitations of the present in order to *believe* that something other than what appears to be real and pragmatic might one day materialise — and probably sooner, and in more forceful ways, than anyone is capable of envisioning at the moment. The alternative, as Mark so passionately argued, is to deceive yourself that there is no alternative — and as he proved beyond doubt, that delusion is as ridiculous as it is damaging to the fate of human life at its most basic level of meaning. In spite of its subtexts of tragedy and frustrated idealism, there seems little doubt that because of this core message, *Capitalist Realism* will have many more days in the sun.

1.

It's easier to imagine the end of the world than the end of capitalism

In one of the key scenes in Alfonso Cuarón's 2006 film *Children of Men*, Clive Owen's character, Theo, visits a friend at Battersea Power Station, which is now some combination of government building and private collection. Cultural treasures – Michelangelo's *David*, Picasso's *Guernica*, Pink Floyd's inflatable pig – are preserved in a building that is itself a refurbished heritage artifact. This is our only glimpse into the lives of the elite, holed up against the effects of a catastrophe which has caused mass sterility: no children have been born for a generation. Theo asks the question, 'how all this can matter if there will be no-one to see it?' The alibi can no longer be future generations, since there will be none. The response is nihilistic hedonism: 'I try not to think about it'.

What is unique about the dystopia in *Children of Men* is that it is specific to late capitalism. This isn't the familiar totalitarian scenario routinely trotted out in cinematic dystopias (see, for example, James McTeigue's 2005 *V for Vendetta*). In the P.D. James novel on which the film is based, democracy is suspended and the country is ruled over by a self-appointed Warden, but, wisely, the film downplays all this. For all that we know, the authoritarian measures that are everywhere in place could have been implemented within a political structure that remains, notionally, democratic. The War on Terror has prepared us for such a development: the normalization of crisis produces a situation in which the repealing of measures brought in to deal with an emergency becomes unimaginable (when will the war be over?)

Watching *Children of Men*, we are inevitably reminded of the phrase attributed to Fredric Jameson and Slavoj Žižek, that it is easier to imagine the end of the world than it is to imagine the end of capitalism. That slogan captures precisely what I mean by 'capitalist realism': the widespread sense that not only is capitalism the only viable political and economic system, but also that it is now impossible even to *imagine* a coherent alternative to it. Once, dystopian films and novels were exercises in such acts of imagination – the disasters they depicted acting as narrative pretext for the emergence of different ways of living. Not so in *Children of Men*. The world that it projects seems more like an extrapolation or exacerbation of ours than an alternative to it. In its world, as in ours, ultra-authoritarianism and Capital are by no means incompatible: internment camps and franchise coffee bars co-exist. In *Children of Men*, public space is abandoned, given over to uncollected garbage and stalking animals (one especially resonant scene takes place inside a derelict school, through which a deer runs). Neoliberals, the capitalist realists par excellence, have celebrated the destruction of public space but, contrary to their official hopes, there is no withering away of the state in *Children of Men*, only a stripping back of the state to its core military and police functions (I say 'official' hopes since neoliberalism surreptitiously relied on the state even while it has ideologically excoriated it. This was made spectacularly clear during the banking crisis of 2008, when, at the invitation of neoliberal ideologues, the state rushed in to shore up the banking system.)

The catastrophe in *Children of Men* is neither waiting down the road, nor has it already happened. Rather, it is being lived through. There is no punctual moment of disaster; the world doesn't end with a bang, it winks out, unravels, gradually falls apart. What caused the catastrophe to occur, who knows; its cause lies long in the past, so absolutely detached from the present as to seem like the caprice of a malign being: a negative miracle, a malediction which no penitence can ameliorate. Such a blight can only be eased by an intervention that can no more be anticipated than was the onset of the curse in the first place. Action is pointless; only senseless hope makes sense. Superstition and religion, the first resorts of the helpless, proliferate.

But what of the catastrophe itself? It is evident that the theme of sterility must be read metaphorically, as the displacement of another kind of anxiety. I want to argue this anxiety cries out to be read in cultural terms, and the question the film poses is: how long can a culture persist without the new? What happens if the young are no longer capable of producing surprises?

Children of Men connects with the suspicion that the end has already come, the thought that it could well be the case that the future harbors only reiteration and re-permutation. Could it be that there are no breaks, no 'shocks of the new' to come? Such anxieties tend to result in a bi-polar oscillation: the 'weak messianic' hope that there must be something new on the way lapses into the morose conviction that nothing new can ever happen. The focus shifts from the Next Big Thing to the last big thing – how long ago did it happen and just how big was it?

T.S. Eliot looms in the background of *Children of Men*, which, after all, inherits the theme of sterility from *The Waste Land*. The film's closing epigraph 'shantih shantih shantih' has more to do with Eliot's fragmentary pieces than the Upanishads' peace. Perhaps it is possible to see the concerns of another Eliot – the Eliot of 'Tradition and the Individual Talent' – ciphered in *Children of Men*. It was in this essay that Eliot, in anticipation of Harold Bloom, described the reciprocal relationship between the canonical and the new. The new defines itself in response to what is already established; at the same time, the established has to reconfigure itself in response to the new. Eliot's claim was that the exhaustion of the future does not even leave us with the past. Tradition counts for nothing when it is no longer

3

contested and modified. A culture that is merely preserved is no culture at all. The fate of Picasso's *Guernica* in the film – once a howl of anguish and outrage against Fascist atrocities, now a wall-hanging – is exemplary. Like its Battersea hanging space in the film, the painting is accorded 'iconic' status only when it is deprived of any possible function or context. No cultural object can retain its power when there are no longer new eyes to see it.

We do not need to wait for *Children of Men*'s near-future to arrive to see this transformation of culture into museum pieces. The power of capitalist realism derives in part from the way that capitalism subsumes and consumes all of previous history: one effect of its 'system of equivalence' which can assign all cultural objects, whether they are religious iconography, pornography, or *Das Kapital*, a monetary value. Walk around the British Museum, where you see objects torn from their lifeworlds and assembled as if on the deck of some Predator spacecraft, and you have a powerful image of this process at work. In the conversion of practices and rituals into merely aesthetic objects, the beliefs of previous cultures are objectively ironized, transformed into *artifacts*. Capitalist realism is therefore not a particular type of realism; it is more like realism in itself. As Marx and Engels themselves observed in *The Communist Manifesto*,

> [Capital] has drowned the most heavenly ecstasies of religious fervor, of chivalrous enthusiasm, of philistine sentimentalism, in the icy water of egotistical calculation. It has resolved personal worth into exchange value, and in place of the numberless indefeasible chartered freedoms, has set up that single, unconscionable freedom — Free Trade. In one word, for exploitation, veiled by religious and political illusions, it has substituted naked, shameless, direct, brutal exploitation.

Capitalism is what is left when beliefs have collapsed at the level of ritual or symbolic elaboration, and all that is left is the consumer-spectator, trudging through the ruins and the relics.

Yet this turn from belief to aesthetics, from engagement to spectatorship, is held to be one of the virtues of capitalist realism. In claiming, as Badiou puts it, to have 'delivered us from the "fatal abstractions" inspired by the "ideologies of the past"', capitalist realism presents itself as a shield protecting us from the perils posed by belief itself. The attitude of ironic distance proper to postmodern capitalism is supposed to immunize us against the seductions of fanaticism. Lowering our expectations, we are told, is a small price to pay for being protected from terror and totalitarianism. 'We live in a contradiction,' Badiou has observed:

a brutal state of affairs, profoundly inegalitarian – where all existence is evaluated in terms of money alone – is presented to us as ideal. To justify their conservatism, the partisans of the established order cannot really call it ideal or wonderful. So instead, they have decided to say that all the rest is horrible. Sure, they say, we may not live in a condition of perfect Goodness. But we're lucky that we don't live in a condition of Evil. Our democracy is not perfect. But it's better than the bloody dictatorships. Capitalism is unjust. But it's not criminal like Stalinism. We let millions of Africans die of AIDS, but we don't make racist nationalist declarations like Milosevic. We kill Iraqis with our airplanes, but we don't cut their throats with machetes like they do in Rwanda, etc.

The 'realism' here is analogous to the deflationary perspective of a depressive who believes that any positive state, any hope, is a dangerous illusion.

5

In their account of capitalism, surely the most impressive since Marx's, Deleuze and Guattari describe capitalism as a kind of dark potentiality which haunted all previous social systems. Capital, they argue, is the 'unnamable Thing', the abomination, which primitive and feudal societies 'warded off in advance'. When it actually arrives, capitalism brings with it a massive desacralization of culture. It is a system which is no longer governed by any transcendent Law; on the contrary, it dismantles all such codes, only to re-install them on an *ad hoc* basis. The limits of capitalism are not fixed by fiat, but defined (and re-defined) pragmatically and improvisationally. This makes capitalism very much like the Thing in John Carpenter's film of the same name: a monstrous, infinitely plastic entity, capable of metabolizing and absorbing anything with which it comes into contact. Capital, Deleuze and Guattari says, is a 'motley painting of everything that ever was'; a strange hybrid of the ultra-modern and the archaic. In the years since Deleuze and Guattari wrote the two volumes of their *Capitalism And Schizophrenia*, it has seemed as if the deterritorializing impulses of capitalism have been confined to finance, leaving culture presided over by the forces of reterritorialization.

This malaise, the feeling that there is nothing new, is itself nothing new of course. We find ourselves at the notorious 'end of history' trumpeted by Francis Fukuyama after the fall of the Berlin Wall. Fukuyama's thesis that history has climaxed with liberal capitalism may have been widely derided, but it is accepted, even assumed, at the level of the cultural unconscious. It should be remembered, though, that even when Fukuyama advanced it, the idea that history had reached a 'terminal beach' was not merely triumphalist. Fukuyama warned that his radiant city would be haunted, but he thought its specters would be Nietzschean rather than Marxian. Some of Nietzsche's most prescient pages are those in which he describes the 'oversaturation of an age with history'. 'It leads an age into a dangerous mood of irony in regard to itself', he wrote in *Untimely Meditations*, 'and subsequently into the even more dangerous mood of cynicism', in which 'cosmopolitan fingering', a detached spectatorialism, replaces engagement and involvement. This is the condition of Nietzsche's Last Man, who has seen everything, but is decadently enfeebled precisely by this excess of (self) awareness.

Fukuyama's position is in some ways a mirror image of Fredric Jameson's. Jameson famously claimed that postmodernism is the 'cultural logic of late capitalism'. He argued that the failure of the future was constitutive of a postmodern cultural scene which, as he correctly prophesied, would become dominated by pastiche and revivalism. Given that Jameson has made a convincing case for the relationship between postmodern culture and certain tendencies in consumer (or post-Fordist) capitalism, it could appear that there is no need for the concept of capitalist realism at all. In some ways, this is true. What I'm calling capitalist realism can be subsumed under the rubric of postmodernism as theorized by Jameson. Yet, despite Jameson's heroic work of clarification, postmodernism remains a hugely contested term, its meanings, appropriately but unhelpfully, unsettled and multiple. More importantly, I would want to argue that some of the processes which Jameson described and analyzed have now become so aggravated and chronic that they have gone through a change in kind.

Ultimately, there are three reasons that I prefer the term capitalist realism to postmodernism. In the 1980s, when Jameson first advanced his thesis about postmodernism, there were still, in name at least, political alternatives to capitalism. What we are dealing with now, however, is a deeper, far more pervasive, sense of exhaustion, of cultural and political sterility. In the 80s, 'Really Existing Socialism' still persisted, albeit in its final phase of collapse. In Britain, the fault lines of class antagonism were fully exposed in an event like the Miners' Strike of 1984–1985, and the defeat of the miners was an important moment in the development of capitalist realism, at least as significant in its symbolic dimension as in its practical effects. The closure of pits was defended precisely on the grounds that keeping them open was not 'economically realistic', and the miners were cast in the role of the last actors in a doomed proletarian romance. The 80s were the period when capitalist realism was fought for and established, when Margaret Thatcher's doctrine that 'there is no alternative' – as succinct a slogan of capitalist realism as you could hope for – became a brutally self-fulfilling prophecy.

Secondly, postmodernism involved some relationship to modernism. Jameson's work on postmodernism began with an interrogation of the idea, cherished by the likes of Adorno, that modernism possessed revolutionary potentials by virtue of its formal innovations alone. What Jameson saw happening instead was the incorporation of modernist motifs into popular culture (suddenly, for example, Surrealist techniques would appear in advertising). At the same time as particular modernist forms were absorbed and commodified, modernism's credos – its supposed belief in elitism and its monological, top-down model of culture – were challenged and rejected in the name of 'difference', 'diversity' and 'multiplicity'. Capitalist realism no longer stages this kind of confrontation with modernism. On the contrary, it takes the vanquishing of modernism for granted: modernism is now something that can periodically return, but only as a frozen aesthetic style, never as an ideal for living.

Thirdly, a whole generation has passed since the collapse of the Berlin Wall. In the 1960s and 1970s, capitalism had to face the problem of how to contain and absorb energies from outside. It now, in fact, has the opposite problem; having all-too successfully incorporated externality, how can it function without an outside it can colonize and appropriate? For most people under twenty in Europe and North America, the lack of alternatives to capitalism is no longer even an issue. Capitalism seamlessly occupies the horizons of the thinkable. Jameson used to report in horror about the ways that capitalism had seeped into the very unconscious; now, the fact that capitalism has colonized the dreaming life of the population is so taken for granted that it is no longer worthy of comment. It would be dangerous and misleading to imagine that the near past was some prelapsarian state rife with political potentials, so it's as well to remember the role that commodification played in the production of culture throughout the twentieth century. Yet the old struggle between *detournement* and recuperation, between subversion and incorporation, seems to have been played out. What we are dealing with now is not the incorporation of materials that previously seemed to possess subversive potentials, but instead, their *precorporation*: the pre-emptive formatting and shaping of desires, aspirations and hopes by capitalist culture. Witness, for instance, the establishment of settled 'alternative' or 'independent' cultural zones, which endlessly repeat older gestures of rebellion and contestation as if for the first time. 'Alternative' and 'independent' don't designate something outside mainstream culture; rather, they are styles, in fact *the* dominant styles, within the mainstream. No-one embodied (and struggled with) this deadlock more than Kurt Cobain and Nirvana. In his dreadful lassitude and objectless rage, Cobain seemed to give wearied voice to the despondency of the generation that had come after history, whose every move was anticipated, tracked, bought and sold before it had even happened. Cobain knew that he was just another piece of spectacle, that nothing runs better on MTV than a protest against MTV; knew that his every move was a cliché scripted in advance, knew that even realizing it is a cliché. The impasse that paralyzed Cobain is precisely the one that Jameson described: like postmodern culture in general, Cobain found himself in 'a world in which stylistic innovation is no longer possible, [where] all that is left is to imitate dead styles, to speak through the masks and with the voices of the styles in the imaginary museum'. Here, even success meant failure, since to succeed would only mean that you were the new meat on which the system could feed. But the high existential angst of Nirvana and Cobain belongs to an older moment; what succeeded them was a pastiche-rock which reproduced the forms of the past without anxiety.

Cobain's death confirmed the defeat and incorporation of rock's utopian and promethean ambitions. When he died, rock was already being eclipsed by hip hop, whose global success has presupposed just the kind of precorporation by capital which I alluded to above. For much hip hop, any 'naïve' hope that youth culture could change anything has been replaced by the hard-headed embracing of a brutally reductive version of 'reality'. 'In hip hop', Simon Reynolds pointed out in a 1996 essay in *The Wire* magazine,

'real' has two meanings. First, it means authentic, uncompromised music that refuses to sell out to the music industry and soften its message for crossover. 'Real' also signifies that the music reflects a 'reality' constituted by late capitalist economic instability, institutionalized racism, and increased surveillance and harassment of youth by the police. 'Real' means the death of the social: it means corporations who respond to increased profits not by raising pay or improving benefits but by .... downsizing (the laying-off the permanent workforce in order to create a floating employment pool of part-time and freelance workers without benefits or job security).

In the end, it was precisely hip hop's performance of this first version of the real – 'the uncompromising' – that enabled its easy absorption into the second, the reality of late capitalist economic instability, where such authenticity has proven highly marketable. Gangster rap neither merely reflects pre-existing social conditions, as many of its advocates claim, nor does it simply cause those conditions, as its critics argue – rather the circuit whereby hip hop and the late capitalist social field feed into each other is one of the means by which capitalist realism transforms itself into a kind of anti-mythical myth. The affinity between hip hop and gangster movies such as *Scarface*, *The Godfather* films, *Reservoir Dogs*, *Goodfellas* and *Pulp Fiction* arises from their common claim to have stripped the world of sentimental illusions and seen it for 'what it really is': a Hobbesian war of all against all, a system of perpetual exploitation and generalized criminality. In hip hop, Reynolds writes, 'To "get real" is to confront a state-of-nature where dog eats dog, where you're either a winner or a loser, and where most will be losers'.

The same neo-noir worldview can be found in the comic books of Frank Miller and in the novels of James Ellroy. There is a kind of machismo of demythologization in Miller and Ellroy's works. They pose as unflinching observers who refuse to prettify the world so that it can be fitted into the supposedly simple ethical binaries of the superhero comic and the traditional crime novel. The 'realism' here is somehow underscored, rather than undercut, by their fixation on the luridly venal – even though the hyperbolic insistence on cruelty, betrayal and savagery in both writers quickly becomes pantomimic. 'In his pitch blackness', Mike Davis wrote of Ellroy in 1992, 'there is no light left to cast shadows and evil becomes a forensic banality. The result feels very much like the actual moral texture of the Reagan-Bush era: a supersaturation of corruption that fails any longer to outrage or even interest'. Yet this very desensitization serves a function for capitalist realism: Davis hypothesized that 'the role of L.A. *noir*' may have been 'to endorse the emergence of *homo reaganus*'.

2

What if you held a protest
and everyone came?

In the cases of gangster rap and Ellroy, capitalist realism takes the form of a kind of super-identification with capital at its most pitilessly predatory, but this need not be the case. In fact, capitalist realism is very far from precluding a certain anti-capitalism. After all, and as Žižek has provocatively pointed out, anti-capitalism is widely disseminated in capitalism. Time after time, the villain in Hollywood films will turn out to be the 'evil corporation'. Far from undermining capitalist realism, this gestural anti-capitalism actually reinforces it. Take Disney/ Pixar's *Wall-E* (2008). The film shows an earth so despoiled that human beings are no longer capable of inhabiting it. We're left in no doubt that consumer capitalism and corporations – or rather one mega-corporation, Buy n Large – is responsible for this depredation; and when we see eventually see the human beings in offworld exile, they are infantile and obese, interacting via screen interfaces, carried around in large motorized chairs, and supping indeterminate slop from cups. What we have here is a vision of control and communication much as Jean Baudrillard understood it, in which subjugation no longer takes the form of a subordination to an extrinsic spectacle, but rather invites us to interact and participate. It seems that the cinema audience is itself the object of this satire, which prompted some right wing observers to recoil in disgust, condemning Disney/Pixar for attacking its own audience. But this kind of irony feeds rather than challenges capitalist realism. A film like *Wall-E* exemplifies what Robert Pfaller has called 'interpassivity': the film performs our anti-capitalism for us, allowing us to continue to consume with impunity. The role of capitalist ideology is not to make an explicit case for something in the way that propaganda does, but to conceal the fact that the operations of capital do not depend on any sort of subjectively assumed belief. It is impossible to conceive of fascism or Stalinism without propaganda – but capitalism can proceed perfectly well, in some ways better, without anyone making a case for it. Žižek's counsel here remains invaluable. 'If the concept of ideology is the classic one in which the illusion is located in knowledge', he argues,

> then today's society must appear post-ideological: the prevailing ideology is that of cynicism; people no longer believe in ideological truth; they do not take ideological propositions seriously. The fundamental level of ideology, however, is not of an illusion masking the real state of things but that of an (unconscious) fantasy structuring our social reality itself. And at this level, we are of course far from being a post-ideological society. Cynical distance is just one way ... to blind ourselves to the structural power of ideological fantasy: even if we do not take things seriously, even if we keep an ironical distance, *we are still doing them.*

Capitalist ideology in general, Žižek maintains, consists precisely in the overvaluing of belief – in the sense of inner subjective attitude – at the expense of the beliefs we exhibit and externalize in our behavior. So long as we believe (in our hearts) that capitalism is bad, we are free to continue to participate in capitalist exchange. According to Žižek, capitalism in general relies on this structure of disavowal. We believe that money is only a meaningless token of no intrinsic worth, yet we *act* as if it has a holy value. Moreover, this behavior precisely depends upon the prior disavowal – we are able to fetishize money in our actions only because we have already taken an ironic distance towards money in our heads.

Corporate anti-capitalism wouldn't matter if it could be differentiated from an authentic anti-capitalist movement. Yet, even before its momentum was stalled by the September 11th attacks on the World Trade Center, the so called anti-capitalist movement seemed also to have conceded too much to capitalist realism. Since it was unable to posit a coherent alternative political-economic model to capitalism, the suspicion was that the actual aim was not to replace capitalism but to mitigate its worst excesses; and, since the form of its activities tended to be the staging of protests rather than political organization, there was a sense that the anti-capitalism movement consisted of making a series of hysterical demands which it didn't expect to be met. Protests have formed a kind of carnivalesque background noise to capitalist realism, and the anti-capitalist protests share rather too much with hyper-corporate events like 2005's Live 8, with their exorbitant demands that politicians legislate away poverty.

Live 8 was a strange kind of protest; a protest that everyone could agree with: who is it who actually wants poverty? And it is not that Live 8 was a 'degraded' form of protest. On the contrary, it was in Live 8 that the logic of the protest was revealed in its purest form. The protest impulse of the 60s posited a malevolent Father, the harbinger of a reality principle that (supposedly) cruelly and arbitrarily denies the 'right' to total enjoyment. This Father has unlimited access to resources, but he selfishly - and senselessly - hoards them. Yet it is not capitalism but protest itself which depends upon this figuration of the Father; and one of the successes of the current global elite has been their avoidance of identification with the figure of the hoarding Father, even though the 'reality' they impose on the young is *substantially harsher* than the conditions they protested against in the 60s. Indeed, it was of course the global elite itself – in the form of entertainers such as Richard Curtis and Bono – which organized the Live 8 event.

To reclaim a real political agency means first of all accepting our insertion *at the level of desire* in the remorseless meat-grinder of Capital. What is being disavowed in the abjection of evil and ignorance onto fantasmatic Others is our own complicity in planetary networks of oppression. What needs to be kept in mind is *both* that capitalism is a hyper-abstract impersonal structure *and* that it would be nothing without our co-operation. The most Gothic description of Capital is also the most accurate. Capital is an abstract parasite, an insatiable vampire and zombie-maker; but the living flesh it converts into dead labor is ours, and the zombies it makes are us. There is a sense in which it simply is the case that the political elite *are* our servants; the miserable service they provide from us is to launder our libidos, to obligingly re-present for us our disavowed desires as if they had nothing to do with us.

The ideological blackmail that has been in place since the original Live Aid concerts in 1985 has insisted that 'caring individuals' could end famine directly, without the need for any kind of political solution or systemic reorganization. It is necessary to act straight away, we were told; politics has to be suspended in the name of ethical immediacy. Bono's Product Red brand wanted to dispense even with the philanthropic intermediary. 'Philanthropy is like hippy music, holding hands', Bono proclaimed. 'Red is more like punk rock, hip hop, this should feel like hard commerce'. The point was not to offer an alternative to capitalism – on the contrary, Product Red's 'punk rock' or 'hip hop' character consisted in its 'realistic' acceptance that capitalism is the only game in town. No, the aim was only to ensure that some of the proceeds of particular transactions went to good causes. The fantasy being that western consumerism, far from being intrinsically implicated in systemic global inequalities, could itself solve them. All we have to do is buy the right products.

Capitalism and the Real

'Capitalist realism' is not an original coinage. It was used as far back as the 1960s by a group of German Pop artists and by Michael Schudson in his 1984 book *Advertising, The Uneasy Persuasion*, both of whom were making parodic references to socialist realism. What is new about my use of the term is the more expansive – even exorbitant – meaning that I ascribe to it. Capitalist realism as I understand it cannot be confined to art or to the quasi-propagandistic way in which advertising functions. It is more like a pervasive *atmosphere*, conditioning not only the production of culture but also the regulation of work and education, and acting as a kind of invisible barrier constraining thought and action.

If capitalist realism is so seamless, and if current forms of resistance are so hopeless and impotent, where can an effective challenge come from? A moral critique of capitalism, emphasizing the ways in which it leads to suffering, only reinforces capitalist realism. Poverty, famine and war can be presented as an inevitable part of reality, while the hope that these forms of suffering could be eliminated easily painted as naive utopianism. Capitalist realism can only be threatened if it is shown to be in some way inconsistent or untenable; if, that is to say, capitalism's ostensible 'realism' turns out to be nothing of the sort.

Needless to say, what counts as 'realistic', what seems possible at any point in the social field, is defined by a series of political determinations. An ideological position can never be really successful until it is naturalized, and it cannot be naturalized while it is still thought of as a value rather than a fact. Accordingly, neoliberalism has sought to eliminate the very category of value in the ethical sense. Over the past thirty years, capitalist realism has successfully installed a 'business ontology' in which it is *simply obvious* that everything in society, including healthcare and education, should be run as a business. As any number of radical theorists from Brecht through to Foucault and Badiou have maintained, emancipatory politics must always destroy the appearance of a 'natural order', must reveal what is presented as necessary and inevitable to be a mere contingency, just as it must make what was previously deemed to be impossible seem attainable. It is worth recalling that what is currently called realistic was itself once 'impossible': the slew of privatizations that took place since the 1980s would have been unthinkable only a decade earlier, and the current political-economic landscape (with unions in abeyance, utilities and railways denationalized) could scarcely have been imagined in 1975. Conversely, what was once eminently possible is now deemed unrealistic. 'Modernization', Badiou bitterly observes, 'is the name for a strict and servile definition of the possible. These 'reforms' invariably aim at making impossible what used to be practicable (for the largest number), and making profitable (for the dominant oligarchy) what did not used to be so'.

At this point, it is perhaps worth introducing an elementary theoretical distinction from Lacanian psychoanalysis which Žižek has done so much to give contemporary currency: the difference between the Real and reality. As Alenka Zupancic explains, psychoanalysis's positing of a reality *principle* invites us to be suspicious of any reality that presents itself as natural. 'The reality principle', Zupancic writes,

> is not some kind of natural way associated with how things are ... The reality principle itself is ideologically mediated; one could even claim that it constitutes the highest form of ideology, the ideology that presents itself as empirical fact (or biological, economic...) necessity (and that we tend

to perceive as non-ideological). It is precisely here that we should be most alert to the functioning of ideology.

For Lacan, the Real is what any 'reality' must suppress; indeed, reality constitutes itself through just this repression. The Real is an unrepresentable X, a traumatic void that can only be glimpsed in the fractures and inconsistencies in the field of apparent reality. So one strategy against capitalist realism could involve invoking the Real, or Reals, underlying the reality that capitalism presents to us.

Environmental catastrophe is one such Real. At one level, to be sure, it might look as if Green issues are very far from being 'unrepresentable voids' for capitalist culture. Climate change and the threat of resource-depletion are not being repressed so much as incorporated into advertising and marketing. What this treatment of environmental catastrophe illustrates is the fantasy structure on which capitalist realism depends: a presupposition that resources are infinite, that the earth itself is merely a husk which capital can at a certain point slough off like a used skin, and that any problem can be solved by the market (In the end, *Wall-E* presents a version of this fantasy – the idea that the infinite expansion of capital is possible, that capital can proliferate without labor – on the off world ship, Axiom, all labor is performed by robots; that the burning up of Earth's resources is only a temporary glitch, and that, after a suitable period of recovery, capital can terraform the planet and recolonize it). Yet environmental catastrophe features in late capitalist culture only as a kind of simulacra, its real implications for capitalism too traumatic to be assimilated into the system. The significance of Green critiques is that they suggest that, far from being the only viable political-economic system, capitalism is in fact primed to destroy the entire human environment. The relationship between capitalism and eco-disaster is neither coincidental nor accidental: capital's 'need of a constantly expanding market', its 'growth fetish', mean that capitalism is by its very nature opposed to any notion of sustainability.

But Green issues are already a contested zone, already a site where politicization is being fought for. In what follows, I want to stress two other aporias in capitalist realism, which are not yet politicized to anything like the same degree. The first is mental health. Mental health, in fact, is a paradigm case of how capitalist realism operates. Capitalist realism insists on treating mental health as if it were a natural fact, like weather (but, then again, weather is no longer a natural fact so much as a political-economic effect). In the 1960s and 1970s, radical theory and politics (Laing, Foucault, Deleuze and Guattari, etc.) coalesced around extreme mental conditions such as schizophrenia, arguing, for instance, that madness was not a natural, but a political, category. But what is needed now is a politicization of much more common disorders. Indeed, it is their very commonness which is the issue: in Britain, depression is now the condition that is most treated by the NHS. In his book *The Selfish Capitalist*, Oliver James has convincingly posited a correlation between rising rates of mental distress and the neoliberal mode of capitalism practiced in countries like Britain, the USA and Australia. In line with James's claims, I want to argue that it is necessary to reframe the growing problem of stress (and distress) in capitalist societies. Instead of treating it as incumbent on individuals to resolve their own psychological distress, instead, that is, of accepting the vast *privatization of stress* that has taken place over the last thirty years, we need to ask: how has it become acceptable that so many people, and especially so many young people, are ill? The 'mental health plague' in capitalist societies would suggest that, instead of being the only social system that works, capitalism is inherently dysfunctional, and that the cost of it appearing to work is very high.

The other phenomenon I want to highlight is bureaucracy. In making their case against socialism, neoliberal ideologues often excoriated the top-down bureaucracy which supposedly led to institutional sclerosis and inefficiency in command economies. With the triumph of neoliberalism, bureaucracy was supposed to have been made obsolete; a relic of an unlamented Stalinist past. Yet this is at odds with the experiences of most people working and living in late capitalism, for whom bureaucracy remains very much a part of everyday life. Instead of disappearing, bureaucracy has changed its form; and this new, decentralized, form has allowed it to proliferate. The persistence of bureaucracy in late capitalism does not in itself indicate that capitalism does not work – rather, what it suggests is that the way in which capitalism does actually work is very different from the picture presented by capitalist realism.

In part, I have chosen to focus on mental health problems and bureaucracy because they both feature heavily in an area of culture which is becoming increasingly dominated by the imperatives of capitalist realism: education. Through most of the current decade, I worked as a lecturer in a Further Education college, and in what follows, I will draw extensively on my experiences there. In Britain, Further Education colleges used to be places which students, often from working class backgrounds, were drawn to if they wanted an alternative to more formal state educational institutions. Ever since Further Education colleges were removed from local authority control in the early 1990s, they have become subject both to 'market' pressures and to government-imposed targets. They have been at the vanguard of changes that would be rolled out through the rest of the education system and public services – a kind of lab in which neoliberal 'reforms' of education have been trialed, and as such, they are the perfect place to begin an analysis of the effects of capitalist realism.

4

Reflexive impotence, immobilization and liberal communism

By contrast with their forebears in the 1960s and 1970s, British students today appear to be politically disengaged. While French students can still be found on the streets protesting against neoliberalism, British students, whose situation is incomparably worse, seem resigned to their fate. But this, I want to argue, is a matter not of apathy, nor of cynicism, but of *reflexive impotence*. They know things are bad, but more than that, they know they can't do anything about it. But that 'knowledge', that reflexivity, is not a passive observation of an already existing state of affairs. It is a self-fulfilling prophecy.

Reflexive impotence amounts to an unstated worldview amongst the British young, and it has its correlate in widespread pathologies. Many of the teenagers I worked with had mental health problems or learning difficulties. Depression is endemic. It is the condition most dealt with by the National Health Service, and is afflicting people at increasingly younger ages. The number of students who have some variant of dyslexia is astonishing. It is not an exaggeration to say that being a teenager in late capitalist Britain is now close to being reclassified as a sickness. This pathologization already forecloses any possibility of politicization. By privatizing these problems – treating them as if they were caused only by chemical imbalances in the individual's neurology and/or by their family background – any question of social systemic causation is ruled out.

Many of the teenage students I encountered seemed to be in a state of what I would call depressive hedonia. Depression is usually characterized as a state of anhedonia, but the condition I'm referring to is constituted not by an inability to get pleasure so much as it by an inability to do anything else *except* pursue pleasure. There is a sense that 'something is missing' – but no appreciation that this mysterious, missing enjoyment can only be accessed *beyond* the pleasure principle. In large part this is a consequence of students' ambiguous structural position, stranded between their old role as subjects of disciplinary institutions and their new status as consumers of services. In his crucial essay 'Postscript on Societies of Control', Deleuze distinguishes between the disciplinary societies described by Foucault, which were organized around the enclosed spaces of the factory, the school and the prison, and the new control societies, in which all institutions are embedded in a dispersed corporation.

Deleuze is right to argue that Kafka is the prophet of distributed, cybernetic power that is typical of Control societies. In *The Trial*, Kafka importantly distinguishes between two types of acquittal available to the accused. Definite acquittal is no longer possible, if it ever was ('we have only legendary accounts of ancient cases [which] provide instances of acquittal'). The two remaining options, then, are (1) 'Ostensible acquittal', in which the accused is to all intents and purposes acquitted, but may later, at some unspecified time, face the charges in full, or (2) 'Indefinite postponement', in which the accused engages in (what they hope is an infinitely) protracted process of legal wrangling, so that the dreaded ultimate judgment is unlikely to be forth-coming. Deleuze observes that the Control societies delineated by Kafka himself, but also by Foucault and Burroughs, operate using indefinite postponement: Education as a lifelong process... Training that persists for as long as your working life continues... Work you take home with you... Working from home, homing from work. A consequence of this 'indefinite' mode of power is that external surveillance is succeeded by internal policing. Control only works if you are complicit with it. Hence the Burroughs figure of the 'Control

Addict': the one who is addicted to control, but also, inevitably, the one who has been taken over, possessed by Control.

Walk into almost any class at the college where I taught and you will immediately appreciate that you are in a post-disciplinary framework. Foucault painstakingly enumerated the way in which discipline was installed through the imposition of rigid body postures. During lessons at our college, however, students will be found slumped on desk, talking almost constantly, snacking incessantly (or even, on occasions, eating full meals). The old disciplinary segmentation of time is breaking down. The carceral regime of discipline is being eroded by the technologies of control, with their systems of perpetual consumption and continuous development.

The system by which the college is funded means that it literally cannot afford to exclude students, even if it wanted to. Resources are allocated to colleges on the basis of how successfully they meet targets on achievement (exam results), attendance and retention of students. This combination of market imperatives with bureaucratically-defined 'targets' is typical of the 'market Stalinist' initiatives which now regulate public services. The lack of an effective disciplinary system has not, to say the least, been compensated for by an increase in student self-motivation. Students are aware that if they don't attend for weeks on end, and/or if they don't produce any work, they will not face any meaningful sanction. They typically respond to this freedom not by pursuing projects but by falling into hedonic (or anhedonic) lassitude: the soft narcosis, the comfort food oblivion of Playstation, all-night TV and marijuana.

Ask students to read for more than a couple of sentences and many – and these are A-level students mind you – will protest that they *can't do it*. The most frequent complaint teachers hear is that *it's boring*. It is not so much the content of the written material that is at issue here; it is the act of reading itself that is deemed to be 'boring'. What we are facing here is not just time-honored teenage torpor, but the mismatch between a post-literate 'New Flesh' that is 'too wired to concentrate' and the confining, concentrational logics of decaying disciplinary systems. To be bored simply means to be removed from the communicative sensation-stimulus matrix of texting, YouTube and fast food; to be denied, for a moment, the constant flow of sugary gratification on demand. Some students want Nietzsche in the same way that they want a hamburger; they fail to grasp – and the logic of the consumer system encourages this misapprehension – that the indigestibility, the difficulty *is* Nietzsche.

An illustration: I challenged one student about why he always wore headphones in class. He replied that it didn't matter, because he wasn't actually playing any music. In another lesson, he was playing music at very low volume through the headphones, without wearing them. When I asked him to switch it off, he replied that even he couldn't hear it. Why wear the headphones without playing music or play music without wearing the headphones? Because the presence of the phones on the ears or the knowledge that the music is playing (even if he couldn't hear it) was a reassurance that the matrix was *still there*, within reach. Besides, in a classic example of interpassivity, if the music was still playing, even if he couldn't hear it, then the player could still enjoy it on his behalf. The use of headphones is significant here – pop is experienced not as something which could have impacts upon public space, but as a retreat into private 'OedIpod' consumer bliss, a walling up against the social.

The consequence of being hooked into the entertainment matrix is twitchy, agitated interpassivity, an inability to concentrate or focus. Students' incapacity to connect current lack of focus with future failure, their inability to synthesize time into any coherent narrative, is symptomatic of more than mere demotivation. It is, in fact, eerily reminiscent of Jameson's analysis in 'Postmodernism and Consumer Society'. Jameson observed there that Lacan's theory of schizophrenia offered a 'suggestive aesthetic model' for understanding the fragmenting of subjectivity in the face of the emerging entertainment-industrial complex. 'With the breakdown of the signifying chain', Jameson summarized, 'the Lacanian schizophrenic is reduced to an experience of pure material signifiers, or, in other words, a series of pure and unrelated presents in time'. Jameson was writing in the late 1980s – i.e. the period in which most of my students were born. What we in the classroom are now facing is a generation born into that ahistorical, anti-mnemonic blip culture – a generation, that is to say, for whom time has always come ready-cut into digital micro-slices.

If the figure of discipline was the worker-prisoner, the figure of control is the debtor-addict. Cyberspatial capital operates by addicting its users; William Gibson recognized that in *Neuromancer* when he had Case and the other cyberspace cowboys feeling insects-under-the-skin strung out when they unplugged from the matrix (Case's amphetamine habit is plainly the substitute for an addiction to a far more abstract speed). If, then, something like attention deficit hyperactivity disorder is a pathology, it is a pathology of late capitalism – a consequence of being wired into the entertainment-control circuits of hypermediated consumer culture. Similarly, what is called dyslexia may in many cases amount to a *post-lexia*. Teenagers process capital's image-dense data very effectively without any need to read - slogan-recognition is sufficient to navigate the net-mobile-magazine informational plane. 'Writing has never been capitalism's thing. Capitalism is profoundly illiterate', Deleuze and Guattari argued in *Anti-Oedipus*. 'Electric language does not go by way of the voice or writing: data processing does without them both'. Hence the reason that many successful business people are dyslexic (but is their post-lexical efficiency a cause or effect of their success?)

Teachers are now put under intolerable pressure to mediate between the post-literate subjectivity of the late capitalist consumer and the demands of the disciplinary regime (to pass examinations etc). This is one way in which education, far from being in some ivory tower safely inured from the 'real world', is the engine room of the reproduction of social reality, directly confronting the inconsistencies of the capitalist social field. Teachers are caught between being facilitator-entertainers and disciplinarian-authoritarians. Teachers want to help students to pass the exams; they want us to be authority figures who tell them what to do. Teachers being interpellated by students as authority figures exacerbates the 'boredom' problem, since isn't anything that comes from the place of authority a priori boring? Ironically, the role of disciplinarian is demanded of educators more than ever at precisely the time when disciplinary structures are breaking down in institutions. With families buckling under the pressure of a capitalism which requires both parents to work, teachers are now increasingly required to act as surrogate parents, instilling the most basic behavioral protocols in students and providing pastoral and emotional support for teenagers who are in some cases only minimally socialized.

It is worth stressing that none of the students I taught had any legal obligation to be at college. They could leave if they wanted to. But the lack of any meaningful employment opportunities, together with cynical encouragement from government means that college seems to be the easier, safer option. Deleuze says that Control societies are based on debt rather than enclosure; but there is a way in which the current education system both indebts *and* encloses students. Pay for your own exploitation, the logic insists – get into debt so you can get the same McJob you could have walked into if you'd left school at sixteen...

Jameson observed that 'the breakdown of temporality suddenly releases [the] present of time from all the activities and intentionalities that might focus it and make it a space of praxis'. But nostalgia for the context in which the old types of praxis operated is plainly useless. That is why French students don't in the end constitute an alternative to British reflexive impotence. That the neoliberal *Economist* would deride French opposition to capitalism is hardly surprising, yet its mockery of French 'immobilization' had a point. 'Certainly the students who kicked off the latest protests seemed to think they were re-enacting the events of May 1968 their parents sprang on Charles de Gaulle', it wrote in its lead article of March 30, 2006.

They have borrowed its slogans ('Beneath the cobblestones, the beach!') and hijacked its symbols (the Sorbonne university). In this sense, the revolt appears to be the natural sequel to [2005]'s suburban riots, which prompted the government to impose a state of emergency. Then it was the jobless, ethnic underclass that rebelled against a system that excluded them. Yet the striking feature of the latest protest movement is that this time the rebellious forces are on the side of conservatism. Unlike the rioting youths in the *banlieues*, the objective of the students and public-sector trade unions is to prevent change, and to keep France the way it is.

It's striking how the practice of many of the immobilizers is a kind of inversion of that of another group who also count themselves heirs of 68: the so called 'liberal communists' such as George Soros and Bill Gates who combine rapacious pursuit of profit with the rhetoric of ecological concern and social responsibility. Alongside their social concern, liberal communists believe that work practices should be (post) modernized, in line with the concept of 'being smart'. As Žižek explains,

Being smart means being dynamic and nomadic, and against centralized bureaucracy; believing in dialogue and cooperation as against central authority; in flexibility as against routine; culture and knowledge as against industrial production; in spontaneous interaction and autopoiesis as against fixed hierarchy.

Taken together, the immobilizers, with their implicit concession that capitalism can only be resisted, never overcome, and the liberal communists, who maintain that the amoral excesses of capitalism must be offset by charity, give a sense of the way in which capitalist realism circumscribes current political possibilities. Whereas the immobilizers retain the form of 68-style protest but in the name of resistance to change, liberal communists energetically embrace newness. Žižek is right to argue that, far from constituting any kind of progressive corrective to official capitalist ideology, liberal communism constitutes the dominant ideology of capitalism now. 'Flexibility', 'nomadism' and 'spontaneity' are the very hallmarks of management in a post-Fordist, Control society. But the problem is that any opposition to flexibility and decentralization risks being self-defeating, since calls for inflexibility and centralization are, to say the least, not likely to be very galvanizing.

In any case, resistance to the 'new' is not a cause that the left can or should rally around. Capital thought very carefully about how to break labor; yet there has still not yet been enough thought about what tactics will work against capital in conditions of post-Fordism, and what *new language* can be innovated to deal with those conditions. It is important to contest capitalism's appropriation of 'the new', but to reclaim the 'new' can't be a matter of adapting to the conditions in which we find ourselves – we've done that rather too well, and 'successful adaptation' is the strategy of managerialism par excellence.

The persistent association of neoliberalism with the term 'Restoration', favored by both Badiou and David Harvey, is an important corrective to the association of capital with novelty.

For Harvey and Badiou, neoliberal politics are not about the new, but a *return* of class power and privilege. '[I]n France,' Badiou has said, "Restoration' refers to the period of the return of the King, in 1815, after the Revolution and Napoleon. We are in such a period. Today we see liberal capitalism and its political system, parliamentarianism, as the only natural and acceptable solutions'. Harvey argues that neoliberalization is best conceived of as a *'political* project to re-establish the conditions for capital accumulation and to restore the power of economic elites'. Harvey demonstrates that, in an era popularly described as 'post-political', class war has continued to be fought, but only by one side: the wealthy. 'After the implementation of neoliberal policies in the late 1970s,' Harvey reveals,

> the share of national income of the top 1 per cent of income earners soared, to reach 15 per cent ... by the end of the century. The top 0.1 per cent of income earners in the US increased their share of the national income from 2 per cent in 1978 to over 6 per cent by 1999, while the ratio of the median compensation of workers to the salaries of CEOs increased from just over 30 to 1 in 1970 to nearly 500 to 1 by 2000. ... The US is not alone in this: the top 1 per cent of income earners in Britain have doubled their share of the national income from 6.5 per cent to 13 per cent since 1982.

As Harvey shows, neoliberals were more Leninist than the Leninists, using think-tanks as the intellectual vanguard to create the ideological climate in which capitalist realism could flourish.

The immobilization model – which amounts to a demand to retain the Fordist/disciplinary regime – could not work in Britain or the other countries in which neoliberalism has already taken a hold. Fordism has definitively collapsed in Britain, and with it the sites around which the old politics were organized. At the end of the control essay, Deleuze wonders what new forms an anti-control politics might take:

> One of the most important questions will concern the ineptitude of the unions: tied to the whole of their history of struggle against the disciplines or within the spaces of enclosure, will they be able to adapt themselves or will they give way to new forms of resistance against the societies of control? Can we already grasp the rough outlines of the coming forms, capable of threatening the joys of marketing? Many young people strangely boast of being "motivated"; they re-request apprenticeships and permanent training. It's up to them to discover what they're being made to serve, just as their elders discovered, not without difficulty, the telos of the disciplines.

What must be discovered is a way out of the motivation/ demotivation binary, so that disidentification from the control program registers as something other than dejected apathy. One strategy would be to shift the political terrain – to move away from the unions' traditional focus on pay and onto forms of discontent specific to post-Fordism. Before we analyse that further, we must consider in more depth what post-Fordism actually is.

5

October 6, 1979: 'Don't let yourself get attached to anything'

'A guy told me one time', says organized crime boss Neil McCauley in Michael Mann's 1995 film *Heat*, 'Don't let yourself get attached to anything you are not willing to walk out on in 30 seconds flat if you feel the heat around the corner'. One of the easiest ways to grasp the differences between Fordism and post-Fordism is to compare Mann's film with the gangster movies made by Francis Ford Coppola and Martin Scorsese between 1971 and 1990. In *Heat*, the scores are undertaken not by Families with links to the Old Country, but by rootless crews, in an LA of polished chrome and interchangeable designer kitchens, of featureless freeways and late-night diners. All the local color, the cuisine aromas, the cultural idiolects which the likes of *The Godfather* and *Goodfellas* depended upon have been painted over and re-fitted. *Heat*'s Los Angeles is a world without landmarks, a branded Sprawl, where markable territory has been replaced by endlessly repeating vistas of replicating franchises. The ghosts of Old Europe that stalked Scorsese and Coppola's streets have been exorcised, buried with the ancient beefs, bad blood and burning vendettas somewhere beneath the multinational coffee shops. You can learn a great deal about the world of *Heat* from considering the name 'Neil McCauley'. It is an anonymous name, a fake passport name, a name that is bereft of history (even as, ironically, it echoes the name of British historian, Lord McCaulay). Compare 'Corleone', and remember that the Godfather was named after a village. McCauley is perhaps the part that De Niro played that is closest to the actor's own personality: a screen, a cipher, depthless, icily professional, stripped down to pure preparation, research, Method ('I do what I do best'). McCauley is no mafia Boss, no puffed-up chief perched atop a baroque hierarchy governed by codes as solemn and mysterious as those of the Catholic Church and written in the blood of a thousand feuds. His Crew are professionals, hands-on entrepreneur-speculators, crime-technicians, whose credo is the exact opposite of *Cosa Nostra* family loyalty. Family ties are unsustainable in these conditions, as McCauley tells the Pacino character, the driven detective, Vincent Hanna. 'Now, if you're on me and you gotta move when I move, how do you expect to keep a marriage?' Hanna is McCauley's shadow, forced to assume his insubstantiality, his perpetual mobility. Like any group of shareholders, McCauley's crew is held together by the prospect of future revenue; any other bonds are optional extras, almost certainly dangerous. Their arrangement is temporary, pragmatic and lateral – they know that they are interchangeable machine parts, that there are no guarantees, that nothing lasts. Compared to this, the goodfellas seem like sedentary sentimentalists, rooted in dying communities, doomed territories.

The ethos espoused by McCauley is the one which Richard Sennett examines in *The Corrosion of Character: The Personal Consequences of Work in the New Capitalism,* a landmark study of the affective changes that the post-Fordist reorganization of work has brought about. The slogan which sums up the new conditions is 'no long term'. Where formerly workers could acquire a single set of skills and expect to progress upwards through a rigid organizational hierarchy, now they are required to periodically re-skill as they move from institution to institution, from role to role. As the organization of work is decentralized, with lateral networks replacing pyramidal hierarchies, a premium is put on 'flexibility'. Echoing McCauley's mockery of Hanna in *Heat* ('How do you expect to keep a marriage?'), Sennett emphasizes the intolerable stresses that these conditions of permanent instability put on family life. The values that family life depends upon – obligation, trustworthiness, commitment – are precisely those which are held to be obsolete in the new capitalism. Yet, with the public sphere under attack and the safety nets that a 'Nanny State' used to provide being dismantled, the family becomes an increasingly important place of respite from the pressures of a world in which instability is a constant. The situation of the family in post-Fordist capitalism is contradictory, in precisely the way that traditional Marxism expected: capitalism requires the family (as an essential means of reproducing and caring for labor power; as a salve for the psychic wounds inflicted by anarchic social-economic conditions), even as it undermines it (denying parents time with children, putting intolerable stress on couples as they become the exclusive source of affective consolation for each other).

According to Marxist economist Christian Marazzi, the switch from Fordism to post-Fordism can be given a very specific date: October 6, 1979. It was on that date that the Federal Reserve increased interest rates by 20 points, preparing the way for the 'supply-side economics' that would constitute the 'economic reality' in which we are now enmeshed. The rise in interest rates not only contained inflation, it made possible a new organization of the means of production and distribution. The 'rigidity' of the Fordist production line gave way to a new 'flexibility', a word that will send chills of recognition down the spine of every worker today. This flexibility was defined by a deregulation of Capital and labor, with the workforce being casualized (with an increasing number of workers employed on a temporary basis), and outsourced.

Like Sennett, Marazzi recognizes that the new conditions both required and emerged from an increased cybernetization of the working environment. The Fordist factory was crudely divided into blue and white collar work, with the different types of labor physically delimited by the structure of the building itself. Laboring in noisy environments, watched over by managers and supervisors, workers had access to language only in their breaks, in the toilet, at the end of the working day, or when they were engaged in sabotage, because communication interrupted production. But in post-Fordism, when the assembly line becomes a 'flux of information', people work by communicating. As Norbert Wiener taught, communication and control entail one another.

Work and life become inseparable. Capital follows you when you dream. Time ceases to be linear, becomes chaotic, broken down into punctiform divisions. As production and distribution are restructured, so are nervous systems. To function effectively as a component of just–in-time production you must develop a capacity to respond to unforeseen events, you must learn to live in conditions of total instability, or 'precarity', as the ugly neologism has it. Periods of work alternate with periods of unemployment. Typically, you find yourself employed in a series of short-term jobs, unable to plan for the future.

Both Marazzi and Sennett point out that the disintegration of stable working patterns was in part driven by the desires of workers – it was they who, quite rightly, did not wish to work in the same factory for forty years. In many ways, the left has never recovered from being wrong-footed by Capital's mobilization and metabolization of the desire for emancipation from Fordist routine. Especially in the UK, the traditional representatives of the working class – union and labor leaders – found Fordism rather too congenial; its stability of antagonism gave them a guaranteed role. But this meant that it was easy for the advocates of post-Fordist Capital to present themselves as the opponents of the status quo, bravely resisting an inertial organized labor 'pointlessly' invested in fruitless ideological antagonism which served the ends of union leaders and politicians, but did little to advance the hopes of the class they purportedly represented. Antagonism is not now located externally, in the face-off between class blocs, but internally, in the psychology of the worker, who, as a worker, is interested in old-style class conflict, but, as someone with a pension fund, is also interested in maximizing the yield from his or her investments. There is no longer an identifiable external enemy. The consequence is, Marazzi argues, that post-Fordist workers are like the Old Testament Jews after they left the 'house of slavery': liberated from a bondage to which they have no wish to return but also abandoned, stranded in the desert, confused about the way forward.

The psychological conflict raging within individuals cannot but have casualties. Marazzi is researching the link between the increase in bi-polar disorder and post-Fordism and, if, as Deleuze and Guattari argue, schizophrenia is the condition that marks the outer edges of capitalism, then bi-polar disorder is the mental illness proper to the 'interior' of capitalism. With its ceaseless boom and bust cycles, capitalism is itself fundamentally and irreducibly bi-polar, periodically lurching between hyped-up mania (the irrational exuberance of 'bubble thinking') and depressive come-down. (The term 'economic depression' is no accident, of course). To a degree unprecedented in any other social system, capitalism both feeds on and reproduces the moods of populations. Without delirium and confidence, capital could not function.

It seems that with post-Fordism, the 'invisible plague' of psychiatric and affective disorders that has spread, silently and stealthily, since around 1750 (i.e. the very onset of industrial capitalism) has reached a new level of acuteness. Here, Oliver James's work is important. In *The Selfish Capitalist*, James points to significant rises in the rates of 'mental distress' over the last 25 years. 'By most criteria', James reports, rates of distress almost doubled between people born in 1946 (aged thirty-six in 1982) and 1970 (aged thirty in 2000). For example, 16 per cent of thirty-six-year-old women in 1982 reported having 'trouble with nerves, feeling low, depressed or sad', whereas 29 per cent of thirty year-olds reported this in 2000 (for men it was 8 per cent in 1982, 13 per cent in 2000).

Another British study James cites compared levels of psychiatric morbidity (which includes neurotic symptoms, phobias and depression) in samples of people in 1977 and 1985. 'Whereas 22 per cent of the 1977 sample reported psychiatric morbidity, this had risen to almost a third of the population (31 per cent) by 1986'. Since these rates are much higher in countries that have implemented what James calls 'selfish' capitalism than in other capitalist nations, James hypothesizes that it is selfish (i.e. neoliberalized) capitalist policies and culture that are to blame. Specifically, James points to the way in which selfish capitalism stokes up

both aspirations and the expectations that they can be fulfilled. ... In the entrepreneurial fantasy society, the delusion is fostered that anyone can be Alan Sugar or Bill Gates, never mind that the actual likelihood of this occurring has diminished since the 1970s – a person born in 1958 was more likely than one born in 1970 to achieve upward mobility through education, for example. The Selfish Capitalist toxins that are most poisonous to well-being are the systematic encouragement of the ideas that material affluence is they key to fulfillment, that only the affluent are winners and that access to the top is open to anyone willing to work hard enough, regardless of their familial, ethnic or social background – if you do not succeed, there is only one person to blame.

James's conjectures about aspirations, expectations and fantasy fit with my own observations of what I have called 'hedonic depression' in British youth.

It is telling, in this context of rising rates of mental illness, that New Labour committed itself, early in its third term in government, to removing people from Incapacity Benefit, implying that many, if not most, claimants are malingerers. In contrast with this assumption, it doesn't seem unreasonable to infer that most of the people claiming Incapacity Benefit – and there are well in excess of two million of them – are casualties of Capital. A significant proportion of claimants, for instance, are people psychologically damaged as a consequence of the capitalist realist insistence that industries such as mining are no longer economically viable. (Even considered in brute economic terms, though, the arguments about 'viability' seem rather less than convincing, especially once you factor in the cost to taxpayers of incapacity and other benefits.) Many have simply buckled under the terrifyingly unstable conditions of post-Fordism.

The current ruling ontology denies any possibility of a social causation of mental illness. The chemico-biologization of mental illness is of course strictly commensurate with its de-politicization. Considering mental illness an individual chemico-biological problem has enormous benefits for capitalism. First, it reinforces Capital's drive towards atomistic individualization (you are sick because of your brain chemistry). Second, it provides an enormously lucrative market in which multinational pharmaceutical companies can peddle their pharmaceuticals (we can cure you with our SSRIs). It goes without saying that all mental illnesses are neurologically *instantiated*, but this says nothing about their *causation*. If it is true, for instance, that depression is constituted by low serotonin levels, what still needs to be explained is why particular individuals have low levels of serotonin. This requires a social and political explanation; and the task of repoliticizing mental illness is an urgent one if the left wants to challenge capitalist realism.

It does not seem fanciful to see parallels between the rising incidence of mental distress and new patterns of assessing workers' performance. We will now take a closer look at this 'new bureaucracy'.

6

All that is solid melts into PR: Market Stalinism and bureaucratic anti-production

Mike Judge's unjustly undercelebrated film *Office Space* (1999) is as acute an account of the 90s/00s workplace as Schrader's *Blue Collar* (1978) was of 70s labor relations. Instead of the confrontation between trade union officials and management in a factory, Judge's film shows a corporation sclerotized by administrative 'anti-production': workers receive multiple memos from different managers saying the exact same thing. Naturally, the memo concerns a bureaucratic practice: it aims to induce compliance with a new procedure of putting 'cover sheets' on reports. In keeping with the 'being smart' ethos, the management style in *Office Space* is a mixture of shirtsleeves-informality and quiet authoritarianism. Judge shows this same managerialism presides in the corporate coffee chains where the office workers go to relax. Here, staff are required to decorate their uniforms with 'seven pieces of flair', (i.e. badges or other personal tokens) to express their 'individuality and creativity': a handy illustration of the way in which 'creativity' and 'self-expression' have become intrinsic to labor in Control societies; which, as Paolo Virno, Yann Moulier Boutang and others have pointed out, now makes affective, as well as productive demands, on workers. Furthermore, the attempt to crudely quantify these affective contributions also tells us a great deal about the new arrangements. The flair example also points to another phenomenon: hidden expectations behind official standards. Joanna, a waitress at the coffee chain, wears exactly seven pieces of flair, but it is made clear to her that, even though seven is *officially* enough, it is *actually* inadequate – the manager asks if she wants to look the sort of person 'who only does the bare minimum.'

'You know what, Stan, if you want me to wear 37 pieces of flair,' Joanna complains, 'why don't you just make the minimum 37 pieces of flair?'

'Well,' the manager replies, 'I thought I remembered you saying that you wanted to express yourself.' Enough is no longer enough. This syndrome will be familiar to many workers who may find that a 'satisfactory' grading in a performance evaluation is no longer satisfactory. In many educational institutions, for instance, if after a classroom observation a teacher is graded as 'satisfactory', they will be required to undertake training prior to a reassessment.

Initially, it might appear to be a mystery that bureaucratic measures should have *intensified* under neoliberal governments that have presented themselves as anti-bureaucratic and anti-Stalinist. Yet new kinds of bureaucracy – 'aims and objectives', 'outcomes', 'mission statements' – have proliferated, even as neoliberal rhetoric about the end of top-down, centralized control has gained pre-eminence. It might seem that bureaucracy is a kind of return of the repressed, ironically re-emerging at the heart of a system which has professed to destroy it. But the resurgence of bureaucracy in neoliberalism is more than an atavism or an anomaly.

As I have already indicated, there is no contradiction between 'being smart' and the increase of administration and regulation: they are two sides of labor in Control societies. Richard Sennett has argued that the flattening of pyramidal hierarchies has actually led to more surveillance of workers. 'One of the claims made for the new organization of work is that it decentralizes power, that is, gives people in the lower ranks of organization more control over their own activities', Sennett writes. 'Certainly this claim is false in terms of the techniques employed for taking apart the old bureaucratic behemoths. The new information systems provide a comprehensive picture of the organization to top managers in ways which give individuals anywhere in the network little room to hide'. But it isn't only that information technology has granted managers more access to data; it is that the data itself has proliferated. Much of this 'information' is provided by workers themselves. Massimo De Angelis and David Harvie describe some of the bureaucratic measures with which a lecturer must comply when putting together a module for an undergraduate degree in British universities. 'For each module', De Angelis and Harvie write,

> the 'module leader' (ML, i.e., lecturer) must complete various paperwork, in particular a 'module specification' (at the module's start) which lists the module's 'aims and objectives', ILOs, 'modes and methods of assessment', amongst other information; and a 'module review' document (at the end of the module), in which the ML reports their own assessment of the module's strengths and weaknesses and their suggested changes for the following year; a summary of student feedback; and average marks and their dispersion.

This is only the beginning, however. For the degree program as a whole, academics must prepare a 'program specification', as well as producing 'annual program reports', which record student performance according to 'progression rates', 'withdrawal rates', location and spread of marks. All students' marks have to be graded against a 'matrix'. This auto-surveillance is complemented by assessments carried out by external authorities. The marking of student assignments is monitored by 'external examiners' who are supposed to maintain consistency of standards across the university sector. Lecturers have to be observed by their peers, while departments are subject to periodic three or four day inspections by the Quality Assurance Agency for Higher Education (QAA). If they are 'research active', lecturers must submit their 'best four publications' every four or five years to be graded by panel as part of the Research Assessment Exercise (replaced in 2008 by the equally controversial Research Excellence Framework). De Angelis and Harvie are clear that these are only very sketchy accounts of only *some* of the bureaucratic tasks that academics have to perform, all of which have funding implications for institutions. This battery of bureaucratic procedures is by no means confined to universities, nor to education: other public services, such as the National Health Service and the police force, find themselves enmeshed in similar bureaucratic metastases.

This is in part a consequence of the inherent resistance of certain processes and services to marketization. (The supposed marketization of education, for instance, rests on a confused and underdeveloped analogy: are students the *consumers* of the service or its *product*?) The idealized market was supposed to deliver 'friction free' exchanges, in which the desires of consumers would be met directly, without the need for intervention or mediation by regulatory agencies. Yet the drive to assess the performance of workers and to measure forms of labor which, by their nature, are resistant to quantification, has inevitably required additional layers of management and bureaucracy. What we have is not a direct comparison of workers' performance or output, but a comparison between the audited *representation* of that performance and output. Inevitably, a short-circuiting occurs, and work becomes geared towards the generation and massaging of representations rather than to the official goals of the work itself. Indeed, an anthropological study of local government in Britain argues that 'More effort goes into ensuring that a local authority's services are represented correctly than goes into actually improving those services'. This reversal of priorities is one of the hallmarks of a system which can be characterized without hyperbole as 'market Stalinism'. What late capitalism repeats from Stalinism is just this valuing of symbols of achievement over actual achievement. As Marshall Berman explained, describing Stalin's White Sea Canal project of 1931-33:

> Stalin seems to have been so intent on creating a highly visible symbol of development that he pushed and squeezed the project in ways that only retarded the *development* of the project. Thus the workers and the engineers were never allowed the time, money or equipment necessary to build a canal that would be deep enough and safe enough to carry twentieth-century cargoes; consequently, the canal has never played any significant role in Soviet commerce or industry. All the canal could support, apparently, were tourist steamers, which in the 1930s were abundantly stocked with Soviet and foreign writers who obligingly proclaimed the glories of the work. The canal was a triumph of publicity; but if half the care that went into the public relations campaign had been devoted to the work itself, there would have been far fewer victims and far more real developments – and the project would have been a genuine tragedy, rather than a brutal farce in which real people were killed by pseudo-events.

In a strange compulsion to repeat, the ostensibly anti-Stalinist neoliberal New Labour government has shown the same tendency to implement initiatives in which real world effects matter only insofar as they register at the level of (PR) appearance. The notorious 'targets' which the New Labour government was so enthusiastic in imposing are a case in point. In a process that repeats itself with iron predictability everywhere that they are installed, targets quickly cease to be a way of measuring performance and become ends in themselves. Anxiety about falling standards in school examinations is now a regular feature of the summertime in Britain. Yet if students are less skilled and knowledgeable than their predecessors, this is due not to a decline in the quality of examinations *per se*, but to the fact that all of the teaching is geared towards passing the exams. Narrowly focused 'exam drill' replaces a wider engagement with subjects. Similarly, hospitals perform many routine procedures instead of a few serious, urgent operations, because this allows them to hit the targets they are assessed on (operating rates, success rates and reduction in waiting time) more effectively.

It would be a mistake to regard this market Stalinism as some deviation from the 'true spirit' of capitalism. On the contrary, it would be better to say that an essential dimension of Stalinism was inhibited by its association with a social project like socialism and can *only* emerge in a late capitalist culture in which images acquire an autonomous force. The way value is generated on the stock exchange depends of course less on what a company 'really does', and more on perceptions of, and beliefs about, its (future) performance. In capitalism, that is to say, all that is solid melts into PR, and late capitalism is defined at least as much by this ubiquitous tendency towards PR-production as it is by the imposition of market mechanisms.

Here, Žižek's elaboration of Lacan's concept of the 'big Other' is crucial. The big Other is the collective fiction, the symbolic structure, presupposed by any social field. The big Other can never be encountered in itself; instead, we only ever confront its stand-ins. These representatives are by no means always leaders. In the example of the White Sea Canal above, for instance, it wasn't Stalin himself who was the representative of the big Other so much as the Soviet and foreign writers who had to be persuaded of the glories of the project. One important dimension of the big Other is that it does not know everything. It is this constitutive ignorance of the big Other that allows public relations to function. Indeed, the big Other could be defined as the consumer of PR and propaganda, the virtual figure which is required to believe even when no individual can. To use one of Žižek's examples: who was it, for instance, who didn't know that Really Existing Socialism (RES) was shabby and corrupt? Not any of the people, who were all too aware of its shortcomings; nor any of the government administrators, who couldn't but know. No, it was the big Other who was the one deemed not to know – who wasn't allowed to know – the quotidian reality of RES. Yet the distinction between what the big Other knows, i.e. what is officially accepted, and what is widely known and experienced by actual individuals, is very far from being 'merely' emptily formal; it is the discrepancy between the two that allows 'ordinary' social reality to function. When the illusion that the big Other did not know can no longer be maintained, the incorporeal fabric holding the social system together disintegrates. This is why Khrushchev's speech in 1965, in which he 'admitted' the failings of the Soviet state, was so momentous. It is not as if anyone in the party was unaware of the atrocities and corruption carried out in its name, but Khrushchev's announcement made it impossible to believe any more that the big Other was ignorant of them.

So much for Really Existing Socialism – but what of Really Existing Capitalism? One way to understand the 'realism' of capitalist realism is in terms of the claim to have given up belief in the big Other. Postmodernism can be construed as the name for the complex of crises that the decline in the belief in the big Other has triggered, as Lyotard's famous formulation of the postmodern condition – 'incredulity towards metanarratives' – suggests. Jameson, of course, would argue that the 'incredulity towards metanarratives' is one expression of the 'cultural logic of late capitalism', a consequence of the switch into the post-Fordist mode of capital accumulation. Nick Land gives one of the most euphoric accounts of the 'postmodern meltdown of culture into the economy'. In Land's work, a cybernetically upgraded invisible hand is progressively eliminating centralized state power. Land's 90s texts synthesized cybernetics, complexity theory, cyberpunk fiction and neoliberalism to construct a vision of capital planetary artificial intelligence: a vast, supple, endlessly fissile system which renders human will obsolete. In his manifesto for nonlinear, decentered Capital, 'Meltdown', Land invokes a 'massively distributed matrix-networked tendency oriented to disabling ROM command-control programs sustaining all macro- and micro-governmental entities, globally concentrating themselves as the Human Security System'. This is capitalism as a shattering Real, in which (viral, digital) signals circulate on self-sustaining networks which bypass the Symbolic, and therefore do not require the big Other as guarantor. It is Deleuze and Guattari's Capital as 'Unnamable Thing', but without the forces of reterritorialization and anti-production which they argued were *constitutive* of capitalism. One of the problems of Land's position is also what is most interesting about it: precisely that it posits a 'pure' capitalism, a capitalism which is only inhibited and blocked by *extrinsic*, rather than internal, elements (according to Land's logic, these elements are atavisms that will eventually be consumed and metabolized by Capital). Yet capitalism cannot be 'purified' in this way; strip away the forces of anti-production and capitalism disappears with them. Similarly, there is no progressive tendency towards an 'unsheathing' of capitalism, no gradual unmasking of Capital as it 'really' is: rapacious, indifferent, inhuman. On the contrary, the essential role of the 'incorporeal transformations' effectuated by PR, branding and advertising in capitalism suggests that, in order to operate effectively, capitalism's rapacity depends upon various forms of sheathing. Really Existing Capitalism is marked by the same division which characterized Really Existing Socialism, between, on the one hand, an official culture in which capitalist enterprises are presented as socially responsible and caring, and, on the other, a widespread awareness that companies are actually corrupt, ruthless, etc. In other words, capitalist postmodernity is not quite as incredulous as it would appear to be, as the jeweler Gerald Ratner famously found to his cost. Ratner precisely tried to circumvent the Symbolic and 'tell it how it is', describing the inexpensive jewelry his shops sold as 'crap' in an after-dinner speech. But the consequence of Ratner making this judgment *official* were immediate, and serious - £500m was wiped off the value of the company and he lost his job. Customers might previously have known that the jewelry Ratners sold was poor quality, but the big Other didn't know; as soon as it did, Ratners collapsed.

Vernacular postmodernism has dealt with the 'crisis of symbolic efficiency' in a far less intense way than Nick Land, through metafictional anxieties about the function of the author, and in television programs or films which expose the mechanisms of their own productions and reflexively incorporate discussions of their own status as commodities. But postmodernism's supposed gestures of demystification do not evince sophistication so much as a certain naivety, a conviction that there were others, in the past, who *really* believed in the Symbolic. In fact, of course, 'symbolic efficiency' was achieved precisely by maintaining a clear distinction between a material-empirical causality, and another, incorporeal causality proper to the Symbolic. Žižek gives the example of a judge: 'I know very well that things are the way I see them, that this person is a corrupted weakling, but I nonetheless treat him respectfully, since he wears the insignia of a judge, so that when he speaks, it is the Law itself which speaks through him'. However, postmodernism's

> cynical reduction to reality ... falls short: when a judge speaks, there is in a way more truth in his words (the words of the Institution of law) than in the direct reality of the person of judge if one limits oneself to what one sees, one

simply misses the point. Lacan aims at this paradox with his 'les non-dupes errent': those who do not allow themselves to be caught in the symbolic deception/fiction, who continue to believe their eyes, are the ones who err most. A cynic who 'believes only his eyes' misses the efficiency of the symbolic fiction, and how it structures our experience of reality.

Much of Baudrillard's work was a commentary on this same effect: the way in which the abolition of the Symbolic led not to a direct encounter with the Real, but to a kind of hemorrhaging *of* the Real. For Baudrillard, phenomena such as fly on the wall documentaries and political opinion polls – both of which claimed to present reality in an unmediated way – would always pose an insoluble dilemma. Did the presence of the cameras affect the behavior of those being filmed? Would the publication of poll results affect the future behavior of voters? Such questions were undecidable, and therefore 'reality' would always be elusive: at the very moment when it seemed that it was being grasped in the raw, reality transformed into what Baudrillard, in a much misunderstood neologism, called 'hyperreality'. Uncannily echoing Baudrillard's fixations, the most successful reality television programs ended up *fusing* fly on the wall documentary elements with interactive polling. In effect, there are two levels of 'reality' in these shows: the unscripted behavior of the 'real life' participants onscreen, and the unpredictable responses of the audience at home, which in turn affect the behavior of the onscreen participants. Yet reality TV is continually haunted by questions about fiction and illusion: are the participants acting, suppressing certain aspects of their personality in order to appear more appealing to us, the audience? And have the audience's votes been accurately registered, or is there some kind of a fix? The slogan that the *Big Brother* TV show uses – 'You decide' – captures perfectly the mode of control by feedback that, according to Baudrillard, has replaced old centralized forms of power. We ourselves occupy the empty seat of power, phoning and clicking in our responses. TV's *Big Brother* had superseded Orwell's Big Brother. We the audience are not subjected to a power that comes from outside; rather, we are integrated into a control circuit that has our desires and preferences as its only mandate – but those desires and preferences are returned to us, no longer as ours, but as the desires of the big Other. Clearly, these circuits are not confined to television: cybernetic feedback systems (focus groups, demographic surveys) are now integral to the delivery of all 'services', including education and government.

This returns us to the issue of post-Fordist bureaucracy. There is of course a close relationship between bureaucracy – the discourse of officialdom – and the big Other. Witness two of Žižek's own examples of the big Other at work: a low-level official who, having not been informed of a promotion, says 'Sorry, I have not yet been properly informed about this new measure, so I can't help you...'; a woman who believed that she was suffering bad luck because of the number of her house, who could not be satisfied by simply repainting a different number herself , because 'it has to be done properly, by the responsible state institution...' We are all familiar with bureaucratic libido, with the enjoyment that certain officials derive from this position of disavowed responsibility ('it's not me, I'm afraid, it's the regulations'). The frustration of dealing with bureaucrats often arises because they themselves can make no decisions; rather, they are permitted only to refer to decisions that have always-already been made (by the big Other). Kafka was the greatest writer on bureaucracy because he saw that this structure of disavowal was inherent to bureaucracy. The quest to reach the ultimate authority who will finally resolve K's official status can never end, because the big Other cannot be encountered in itself: there are only officials, more or less hostile, engaged in acts of interpretation about the big Other's intentions. And these acts of interpretation, these deferrals of responsibility, are all that the big Other is.

If Kafka is valuable as a commentator on totalitarianism, it is by revealing that there was a dimension of totalitarianism which cannot be understood on the model of despotic command. Kafka's purgatorial vision of a bureaucratic labyrinth without end chimes with Žižek's claim that the Soviet system was an 'empire of signs', in which even the Nomenklatura themselves – including Stalin and Molotov – were engaged in interpreting a complex series of social semiotic signals. No-one *knew* what was required; instead, individuals could only guess what particular gestures or directives meant. What happens in late capitalism, when there is no possibility of appealing, even in principle, to a final authority which can offer the definitive official version, is a massive intensification of that ambiguity. As an example of this syndrome, let us turn once more to Further Education. At a meeting between Trade Union officials, college Principals and Members of Parliament, the Learning and Skills Council (LSC), the quango at the heart of the FE funding labyrinth, came in for particular attack. Neither the teachers, nor the Principals, nor the MPs could determine how particular directives had generated themselves, since they are not there in government policy itself. The answer was that the LSC 'interpreted' the instructions issued by the Department for Education and Skills. These interpretations then achieve the strange autonomy peculiar to bureaucracy. On the one hand, bureaucratic procedures float freely, independent of any external authority; but that very autonomy means that they assume a heavy implacability, a resistance to any amendment or questioning.

The proliferation of auditing culture in post Fordism indicates that the demise of the big Other has been exaggerated. Auditing can perhaps best be conceived of as fusion of PR and bureaucracy, because the bureaucratic data is usually intended to fulfill a promotional role: in the case of education, for example, exam results or research ratings augment (or diminish) the prestige of particular institutions. The frustration for the teacher is that it seems as if their work is increasingly aimed at impressing the big Other which is collating and consuming this 'data'. 'Data' has been put in inverted commas here, because much of the so-called information has little meaning or application outside the parameters of the audit: as Eeva Berglund puts it, 'the information that audit creates does have consequences even though it is so shorn of local detail, so abstract, as to be misleading or meaningless – except, that is, by the aesthetic criteria of audit itself'.

New bureaucracy takes the form not of a specific, delimited function performed by particular workers but invades all areas of work, with the result that – as Kafka prophesied – workers become their own auditors, forced to assess their own performance. Take, for example, the 'new system' that OFSTED (Office for Standards in Education) uses to inspect Further Education colleges. Under the old system, a college would have a 'heavy' inspection once every four years or so, i.e. one involving many lesson observations and a large number of inspectors present in the college. Under the new, 'improved' system, if a college can demonstrate that its internal assessment systems are effective, it will only have to undergo a 'light' inspection. But the downside of this 'light' inspection is obvious – surveillance and monitoring are outsourced from OFSTED to the college and ultimately to lecturers themselves, and become a permanent feature of the college structure (and of the psychology of individual lecturers). The difference between the old/heavy and new/light inspection system corresponds precisely to Kafka's distinction between ostensible acquittal and indefinite postponement, outlined above. With ostensible acquittal, you petition the lower court judges until they grant you a non-binding reprieve. You are then free from the court, until the time when your case is re-opened. Indefinite postponement, meanwhile, keeps your case at the lowest level of the court, but at the cost of an anxiety that never ends. (The changes in OFSTED inspections are mirrored by the change from the Research Assessment Exercise to the Research Excellence Framework in higher education: periodic assessment will be superseded by a permanent and ubiquitous measurement which cannot help but generate the same perpetual anxiety.)

In any case, it is not as if the 'light' inspection is in any sense preferable for staff than the heavy one. The inspectors are in the college for the same amount of time as they were under the old system. The fact that there are fewer of them does nothing to alleviate the stress of the inspection, which has far more to do with the extra bureaucratic window-dressing one has to do in anticipation of a possible observation than it has to do with any actual observation itself. The inspection, that is to say, corresponds precisely to Foucault's account of the virtual nature of surveillance in *Discipline And Punish*. Foucault famously observes there that there is no need for the place of surveillance to actually be occupied. The effect of not knowing whether you will be observed or not produces an introjection of the surveillance apparatus. You constantly act as if you are always about to be observed. Yet, in the case of school and university inspections, what you will be graded on is not primarily your abilities as a teacher so much as your diligence as a bureaucrat. There are other bizarre effects. Since OFSTED is now observing the college's self-assessment systems, there is an implicit incentive for the college to grade itself and its teaching lower than it actually deserves. The result is a kind of postmodern capitalist version of Maoist confessionalism, in which workers are required to engage in constant symbolic self-denigration. At one point, when our line manager was extolling the virtues of the new, light inspection system, he told us that the problem with our departmental log-books was that they were not sufficiently self-critical. But don't worry, he urged, any self-criticisms we make are purely symbolic, and will never be acted upon; as if performing self-flagellation as part of a purely formal exercise in cynical bureaucratic compliance were any less demoralizing.

In the post-Fordist classroom, the reflexive impotence of the students is mirrored by reflexive impotence of the teachers. De Angelis and Harvie report that

> practices and requirements of standardisation and surveillance obviously impose a huge burden of work on academics and few are happy about it. There have been a number of responses. Managers have frequently suggested there is no alternative (TINA) and have perhaps suggested that what we need to do is 'work smarter, not harder'. This seductive slogan, introduced to dampen staff resistance to further change which in their (our) experience has devastating effects on working conditions, attempts to couple the need for 'change' (restructuring and innovation) in order to meet the budget pressure and increase 'competitiveness', with staff's resistance not only to worsening of their condition of work, but also to the educational and academic 'meaninglessness' of the 'changes'.

The invocation of the idea that 'there is no alternative', and the recommendation to 'work smarter, not harder', shows how capitalist realism sets the tone for labor disputes in post-Fordism. Ending the inspection regime, one lecturer sardonically remarked, seems more impossible than ending slavery was. Such fatalism can only be challenged if a new (collective) political subject emerges.

'...if you can watch the overlap of one reality with another': capitalist realism as dreamwork and memory disorder

'Being realistic' may once have meant coming to terms with of a reality experienced as solid and immovable. Capitalist realism, however, entails subordinating oneself to a reality that is infinitely plastic, capable of reconfiguring itself at any moment. We are confronted with what Jameson, in his essay 'The Antimonies Of The Postmodern', calls 'a purely *fungible* present in which space and psyches alike can be processed and remade at will'. The 'reality' here is akin to the multiplicity of options available on a digital document, where no decision is final, revisions are always possible, and any previous moment can be recalled at any time. The middle manager I referred to above turned adaptation to this 'fungible' reality it into a fine art. He asserted with full confidence a story about the college and its future one day – what the implications of the inspection were likely to be; what senior management was thinking; then *literally the next day* would happily propound a story that directly contradicted what he previously said. There was never a question of his *repudiating* the previous story; it was as if he, only dimly remembered there ever being another story. This, I suppose, is 'good management'. It is, also, perhaps the only way to stay healthy amidst capitalism's perpetual instability. On the face of it, this manager is a model of beaming mental health, his whole being radiating a hail-fellow-well-met bonhomie. Such cheerfulness can only be maintained if one has a near-total absence of any critical reflexivity and a capacity, as he had, to cynically comply with every directive from bureaucratic authority. The *cynicism* of the compliance is essential, of course; the preservation of his 60s liberal self-image depended upon his 'not really believing' in the auditing processes he so assiduously enforced. What this disavowal depends upon is the distinction between inner subjective attitude and outward behavior I discussed above: in terms of his inner subjective attitude, the manager is hostile, even contemptuous, towards, the bureaucratic procedures he supervises; but in terms of his outward behavior, he is perfectly compliant. Yet it is precisely workers' subjective disinvestment from auditing tasks which enables them to continue to perform labor that is pointless and demoralizing.

The manager's capacity to smoothly migrate from one reality to another reminded me of nothing so much as Ursula Le Guin's *The Lathe of Heaven*. It is a novel about George Orr, a man whose dreams literally come true. In time-honored fairy tale fashion, however, the acts of wish fulfillment quickly become traumatic and catastrophic. When, for instance, Orr is induced by his therapist, Dr Haber, into dreaming that the problem of overpopulation is solved, he wakes to find himself in a world in which billions have been wiped out by a plague; a plague that, as Jameson put it in his discussion of the novel, was 'a hitherto non-existent event which rapidly finds its place in our chronological memory of the recent past'. Much of the power of the novel consists in its rendering of these retrospective confabulations, whose mechanics are at once so familiar – because we perform them every night when we dream – and so odd. How could it ever be possible for us to believe successive or even co-extensive stories that so obviously contradict one another? Yet we know from Kant, Nietzsche and psychoanalysis that *waking*, as much as dreaming, experience, depends upon just such screening narratives. If the Real is unbearable, *any* reality we construct must be a tissue of inconsistencies. What differentiates Kant, Nietzsche and Freud from the tiresome cliché that 'life is but a dream' is the sense that the confabulations we live are consensual. The idea that the world we experience is a solipsistic delusion projected from the interior of our mind consoles rather than disturbs us, since it conforms with our infantile fantasies of omnipotence; but the thought that our so-called interiority owes its existence to a fictionalized consensus will always carry an uncanny charge. This extra level of uncanniness is registered in *The Lathe of Heaven* when Le Guin has Orr's reality-warping dreams witnessed by others – the therapist, Haber, who seeks to manipulate and control Orr's ability, and the lawyer, Heather Lelache. What, then, is it like to live through *someone else's* dream coming true?

> [Haber] could not go on talking. He felt it: the shift, the arrival, the change.
>
> The woman felt it too. She looked frightened. Holding the brass necklace up close to her throat like a talisman, she was staring in dismay, shock, terror, out of the window at the view.
>
> [...] What would it do to the woman? Would she understand, would she go mad, what would she do? Would she keep both memories, as he did, the true one and the new one, the old one and the true one?

Does she 'go crazy'? No, not at all: after a few moments of bewildered fugue, Heather Lelache accepts the 'new' world as the 'true' world, editing out the point of suture. This strategy – of accepting the incommensurable and the senseless without question – has always been the exemplary technique of sanity as such, but it has a special role to play in late capitalism, that 'motley painting of everything that ever was', whose dreaming up and junking of social fictions is nearly as rapid as its production and disposal of commodities.

In these conditions of ontological precarity, forgetting becomes an adaptive strategy. Take the example of Gordon Brown, whose expedient reinvention of his political identity involved an attempt to induce a collective forgetting. In an article in *International Socialism*, John Newsinger remembers how

> Brown told the Confederation of British Industry conference that 'business is in my blood'. His mother had been a company director and 'I was brought up in an atmosphere where I knew exactly what was happening as far as business was concerned'. He was, indeed he had always been, one of them. The only problem is that it was not true. As his mother subsequently admitted, she would never have called herself 'a business woman': she had only ever done some 'light administrative duties' for 'a small family firm' and had given up the job when she married, three years before young Gordon was even born. While there have been Labor politicians who have tried to invent working class backgrounds for themselves before, Brown is the first to try and invent a capitalist background.

Newsinger contrasts Brown with his rival and predecessor as British prime minister, Tony Blair, a very different case. While Blair – who presented the strange spectacle of a postmodern messianism – never had any beliefs that he had to recant on, Brown's move from Presbyterian socialist to New Labour supremo was a long, arduous and painful process of repudiation and denial. 'Whereas, for Blair, the embrace of neoliberalism involved no great personal struggle because he had no previous beliefs to dispose of', Newsinger writes, 'for Brown it involved a deliberate decision to change sides. The effort, one suspects, damaged his personality'. Blair was the Last Man by nature and inclination; Brown has become the Last Man, the dwarf at the End of History, by force of will.

Blair was the man without a chest, the outsider the party needed in order to get into power, his joker hysterical face salesman-smooth; Brown's implausible act of self-reinvention is what the party itself had to go through, his fake-smile grimace the objective correlative of Labour's real state now that it has completely capitulated to capitalist realism: gutted, and gutless, its insides replaced by simulacra which once looked lustrous but now possess all the allure of decade-old computer technology.

In conditions where realities and identities are upgraded like software, it is not surprising that memory disorders should have become the focus of cultural anxiety – see, for instance, the *Bourne* films, *Memento*, *Eternal Sunshine Of the Spotless Mind*. In the Bourne films, Jason Bourne's quest to regain his identity goes alongside a continual flight from any settled sense of self. 'Try to understand me... ,' says Bourne in the original novel by Robert Ludlum,

> I have to know certain things ... enough to make a decision... but maybe not everything. A part of me has to be able to walk away, disappear. I have to be able to say to myself, what was isn't any longer, and there's a possibility that it *never* was because I have no memory of it. What a person can't remember didn't exist.... for him.

In the films, Bourne's transnational nomadism is rendered in an ultra-fast cutting style which functions as a kind of anti-memory, pitching the viewer into the vertiginous 'continuous present' which Jameson argues is characteristic of postmodern temporality. The complex plotting of Ludlum's novels is transformed into a series of evanescent event-ciphers and action set pieces which barely cohere into an intelligible narrative. Bereft of personal history, Bourne lacks *narrative* memory, but retains what we might call *formal* memory: a memory – of techniques, practices, actions – that is literally embodied in a series of physical reflexes and tics. Here, Bourne's damaged memory echoes the postmodern nostalgia mode as described by Fredric Jameson, in which contemporary or even futuristic reference at the level of content obscure a reliance on established or antiquated models at the level of form. On the one hand, this is a culture that privileges only the present and the immediate – the extirpation of the long term extends backwards as well as forwards in time (for example, media stories monopolize attention for a week or so then are instantly forgotten); on the other hand, it is a culture that is excessively nostalgic, given over to retrospection, incapable of generating any authentic novelty. It may be that Jameson's identification and analysis of this temporal antimony is his most important contribution to our understanding of postmodern/post-Fordist culture. '[T]he paradox from which we must set forth,' he argues in 'Antimonies Of The Postmodern',

> is the equivalence between an unparalleled rate of change on all the levels of social life and an unparalleled standardization of everything – feelings along with consumer goods, language along with built space – that would seem incompatible with such mutability... What then dawns is the realization that no society has ever been as standardized as this one, and that the stream of human, social and historical temporality has never flowed quite so homogenously. ... What we now begin to feel, therefore – and what begins to emerge as some deeper and more fundamental constitution of postmodernity itself, at least in its temporal dimension – is henceforth, where everything now submits to the perpetual change of fashion and media image, that nothing can change any longer.

No doubt this is another example of the struggle between the forces of deterritorialization and reterritorialization which Deleuze and Guattari argue is constitutive of capitalism as such. It wouldn't be surprising if profound social and economic instability resulted in a craving for familiar cultural forms, to which we return in the same way that Bourne reverts to his core reflexes. The memory disorder that is the correlative of this situation is the condition which afflicts Leonard in *Memento*, theoretically pure anterograde amnesia. Here, memories prior to the onset of the condition are left intact, but sufferers are unable to transfer new memories into long term memory; the new therefore looms up as hostile, fleeting, un-navigable, and the sufferer is drawn back to the security of the old. The *inability to make new memories*: a succinct formulation of the postmodern impasse....

If memory disorder provides a compelling analogy for the glitches in capitalist realism, the model for its smooth functioning would be dreamwork. When we are dreaming, we forget, but immediately forget that we have done so; since the gaps and lacunae in our memories are Photoshopped out, they do not trouble or torment us. What dreamwork does is to produce a confabulated consistency which covers over anomalies and contradictions, and it is this which Wendy Brown picked up on when she argued that it was precisely dreamwork which provided the best model for understanding contemporary forms of power. In her essay 'American Nightmare: Neoconservatism, Neoliberalism, and De-democratization', Brown unpicked the alliance between neoconservatism and neoliberalism which constituted the American version of capitalist realism up until 2008. Brown shows that neoliberalism and neoconservatism operated from premises which are not only inconsistent, but directly contradictory. 'How', Brown asks,

> does a rationality that is expressly amoral at the level of both ends and means (neoliberalism) intersect with one that is expressly moral and regulatory (neoconservatism)? How does a project that empties the world of meaning, that cheapens and deracinates life and openly exploits desire, intersect one centered on fixing and enforcing meanings, conserving certain ways of life, and repressing and regulating desire?

How does support for governance modeled on the firm and a normative social fabric of self-interest marry or jostle against support for governance modeled on church authority and a normative social fabric of self-sacrifice and long-term filial loyalty, the very fabric shredded by unbridled capitalism?

But incoherence at the level of what Brown calls 'political rationality' does nothing to prevent symbiosis at the level of political subjectivity, and, although they proceeded from very different guiding assumptions, Brown argues that neoliberalism and neoconservatism worked together to undermine the public sphere and democracy, producing a governed citizen who looks to find solutions in products, not political processes. As Brown claims,

> the choosing subject and the governed subject are far from opposites ... Frankfurt school intellectuals and, before them, Plato theorized the open compatibility between individual choice and political domination, and depicted democratic subjects who are available to political tyranny or authoritarianism precisely because they are absorbed in a province of choice and need-satisfaction that they mistake for freedom.

Extrapolating a little from Brown's arguments, we might hypothesize that what held the bizarre synthesis of neoconservatism and neoliberalism together was their shared objects of abomination: the so called Nanny State and its dependents. Despite evincing an anti-statist rhetoric, neoliberalism is in practice not opposed to the state *per se* – as the bank bail-outs of 2008 demonstrated – but rather to particular uses of state funds; meanwhile, neoconservatism's strong state was confined to military and police functions, and defined itself against a welfare state held to undermine individual moral responsibility.

8

'There's no central exchange'

Although excoriated by both neoliberalism and neoconservativism, the concept of the Nanny State continues to haunt capitalist realism. The specter of big government plays an essential *libidinal* function for capitalist realism. It is there to be blamed precisely for its *failure* to act as a centralizing power, the anger directed at it much like the fury Thomas Hardy supposedly spat at God for not existing. 'Time and again', James Meek observed in an LRB piece on water privatization in Britain, 'Conservative and Labor governments have discovered that when they give powers to private companies, and those private companies screw up, voters blame the government for giving the powers away, rather than the companies for misusing them'. Meek was visiting Tewkesbury, one of the British towns that was the victim of serious flooding in 2007, a year after the disaster. On the face of it, the flooding and the consequent failure of services was the fault of privatized water companies and house builders, yet Meek found that this was not the way that most of the local residents saw it. 'In Tewkesbury', Meeks wrote,

> in general there is more hostility towards the government, the council and the Environment Agency for not stopping house builders than there is towards house builders for building houses, or buyers for buying them. When insurers raise their premiums, more blame is directed at the government for not spending enough on flood defences than at insurers for raising the premiums, or at people who choose to live in a flood-prone valley but don't like paying extra for it.

This syndrome was repeated on a much grander scale with a disaster of a different kind – the bank crisis of 2008. The media focus was on the excesses of individual bankers and on the government's handling of the crisis, not on the systemic causes of the crisis. I don't for a moment want to excuse New Labour for its part in such disasters, but it has to be recognized that focus on government, like the focus on immoral individuals, is an act of deflection. Scapegoating an impotent government (running around to clean up the messes made by its business friends) arises from bad faith, from a continuing hostility to the Nanny State that nevertheless goes alongside a refusal to accept the consequences of the sidelining of government in global capitalism – a sign, perhaps, that, at the level of the political unconscious, it is impossible to accept that there are no overall controllers, that the closest thing we have to ruling powers now are nebulous, unaccountable interests exercising corporate irresponsibility. A case of fetishist disavowal, perhaps – 'we know perfectly well that the government is not pulling the strings, but nevertheless...' The disavowal happens in part because the centerlessness of global capitalism is radically unthinkable. Although people are interpellated now as consumers – and, as Wendy Brown and others have pointed out, government itself is presented as a kind of commodity or service – they still cannot help but think of themselves as (if they were) citizens.

The closest that most of us come to a direct experience of the centerlessness of capitalism is an encounter with the call center. As a consumer in late capitalism, you increasingly exist in two, distinct realities: the one in which the services are provided without hitch, and another reality entirely, the crazed Kafkaesque labyrinth of call centers, a world without memory, where cause and effect connect together in mysterious, unfathomable ways, where it is a miracle that anything ever happens, and you lose hope of ever passing back over to the other side, where things seem to function smoothly. What exemplifies the failure of the neoliberal world to live up to its own PR better than the call center? Even so, the universality of bad experiences with call centers does nothing to unsettle the operating assumption that capitalism is inherently efficient, as if the problems with call centers weren't the systemic consequences of a logic of Capital which means organizations are so fixated on making profits that they can't actually sell you anything.

The call center experience distils the political phenomenology of late capitalism: the boredom and frustration punctuated by cheerily piped PR, the repeating of the same dreary details many times to different poorly trained and badly informed operatives, the building rage that must remain impotent because it can have no legitimate object, since – as is very quickly clear to the caller – there is no-one who knows, and no-one who could do anything even if they could. Anger can only be a matter of venting; it is aggression in a vacuum, directed at someone who is a fellow victim of the system but with whom there is no possibility of communality. Just as the anger has no proper object, it will have no effect. In this experience of a system that is unresponsive, impersonal, centerless, abstract and fragmentary, you are as close as you can be to confronting the artificial stupidity of Capital in itself.

Call center angst is one more illustration of the way that Kafka is poorly understood as exclusively a writer on totalitarianism; a decentralized, market Stalinist bureaucracy is far more Kafkaesque than one in which there is a central authority. Read, for instance, the bleak farce of K's encounter with the telephone system in the Castle, and it is hard not to see it as uncannily prophetic of the call center experience.

> There's no fixed exchange with the Castle, no central exchange which transmits our calls further. When anybody calls up the Castle from here the instruments in all the subordinate departments ring, or rather they would ring if

practically all the departments – I know this for a certainty – didn't leave their receivers off. Now and then, however, a fatigued official may feel the need of a little distraction, especially in the evenings and at night and may hang the receiver on. Then we get an answer, but of course an answer that's a practical joke. And that's very understandable too. For who would take the responsibility of interrupting, in the middle of the night, the extremely important work that goes on furiously the whole time, with a message about his own private troubles? I can't comprehend how even a stranger can imagine that when he calls up Sordini, for example, it's Sordini that answers.

K's response anticipates the bewildered frustration of the individual in the call center labyrinth. Although many of the conversations with call center operatives appear Dadaistically nonsensical, they cannot be treated as such, cannot be dismissed as being of no significance.

'I didn't know it was like that, certainly,' said K. 'I couldn't know of all these peculiarities, but I didn't put much confidence in those telephone conversations and I was always aware that the only things of any importance were those that happened in the Castle itself.'
'No,' said the Superintendent, holding firmly onto the word, 'these telephone replies from the Castle certainly have a meaning, why shouldn't they? How could a message given by an official from the Castle not be important?'

The supreme genius of Kafka was to have explored the *negative atheology* proper to Capital: the centre is missing, but we cannot stop searching for it or positing it. It is not that there is nothing there – it is that what *is* there is not capable of exercising responsibility.

This problem is addressed from another angle in a paper by Campbell Jones entitled 'The Subject Supposed To Recycle'. In posing the question, *who* is the subject supposed to recycle?' Jones denaturalizes an imperative that is now so taken for granted that resisting it seems senseless, never mind unethical. *Everyone* is supposed to recycle; *no-one*, whatever their political persuasion, ought to resist this injunction. The demand that we recycle is precisely posited as a pre- or post-ideological imperative; in other words, it is positioned in precisely the space where ideology always does its work. But the subject supposed to recycle, Jones argued, presupposed the structure not supposed to recycle: in making recycling the responsibility of 'everyone', structure contracts out its responsibility to consumers, by itself receding into invisibility. Now, when the appeal to individual ethical responsibility has never been more clamorous – in her book *Frames Of War*, Judith Butler uses the term 'responsibilization' to refer to this phenomenon – it is necessary to wager instead on structure at its most totalizing. Instead of saying that *everyone* – i.e. every *one* – is responsible for climate change, we all have to do our bit, it would be better to say that no-one is, and that's the very problem. The cause of eco-catastrophe is an impersonal structure which, even though it is capable of producing all manner of effects, is precisely not a subject capable of exercising responsibility. The required subject – a collective subject – does not exist, yet the crisis, like all the other global crises we're now facing, demands that it be constructed. Yet the appeal to ethical immediacy that has been in place in British political culture since at least 1985 – when the consensual sentimentality of Live Aid replaced the antagonism of the Miners Strike – permanently defers the emergence of such a subject.

Similar issues are touched on in a paper by Armin Beverungen on Alan Pakula's 1974 film *The Parallax View*, which sees *The Parallax View* as providing a kind of diagram of the way in which a certain model of (business) ethics goes wrong. The problem is that the model of individual responsibility assumed by most versions of ethics have little purchase on the behavior of Capital or corporations. *The Parallax View* is in a sense a meta-conspiracy film: a film not only about conspiracies but about the impotence of attempts to uncover them; or, much worse than that, about the way in which particular kinds of investigation feed the very conspiracies they intend to uncover. It is not only that the Warren Beatty character is framed/killed for the crime he is investigating, neatly eliminating him and undermining his investigations with one pull of a corporate assassins trigger; it's that, as Jameson noted in his commentary on the film in *The Geopolitical Aesthetic*, his very tenacity, quasi-sociopathic individualism, make him eminently frameable.

The terrifying climactic moment of *The Parallax View* – when the silhouette of Beatty's anonymous assassin appears against migraine-white space – for me now rhymes with the open door at the end of a very different film, Peter Weir's *The Truman Show*. But where the door in the horizon opening onto black space at the end of Weir's film connotes a break in a universe of total determinism, the nothingness on which existentialist freedom depends, *The Parallax View*'s 'final open door ... opens onto a world conspiratorially organized and controlled as far as the eye can see' (Jameson). This anonymous figure with a rifle in a doorway is the closest we get to seeing the conspiracy (as) itself. The conspiracy in *The Parallax View* never gives any account of itself. It is never focalised through a single malign individual. Although presumably corporate, the interests and motives of the conspiracy in *The Parallax View* are never articulated (perhaps not even to or by those actually involved in it). Who knows what the Parallax Corporation really wants? It is itself situated in the parallax between politics and economy. Is it a commercial front for political interests, or is the whole machinery of government a front for it? It's not clear if the Corporation really exists – more than that, it is not clear if its aim is to pretend that it doesn't exist, or to pretend that it does.

There are certainly conspiracies in capitalism, but the problem is that they are themselves only possible because of deeper level structures that allow them to function. Does anyone really think, for instance, that things would improve if we replaced the whole managerial and banking class with a whole new set of ('better') people? Surely, on the contrary, it is evident that the vices are engendered by the structure, and that while the structure remains, the vices will reproduce themselves. The strength of Pakula's film is precisely to invoke the shadowy, centerless impersonality proper to a corporate conspiracy. As Jameson observes, what Pakula captures so well in *The Parallax View* is a particular kind of corporate affective tonality:

> For the agents of conspiracy, *Sorge* [concern] is a matter of smiling confidence, and the preoccupation is not personal but corporate, concern for the vitality of the network or the institution, a disembodied distraction or inattentiveness engaging the absent space of the collective organization itself without the clumsy conjectures that sap the energies of the victims. These people *know*, and are therefore able to invest their presence as characters in an intense yet complacent attention whose centre of gravity is elsewhere: a rapt intentness which is at the same time disinterest. Yet this very different type of concern, equally depersonalised, carries its own specific anxiety with it, as it were unconsciously and corporately, without any consequences for the individual villains.

... without any consequences for the individual villains... How *that* phrase resonates just now – after the deaths of Jean Charles De Menezes and Ian Tomlinson and after the banking fiasco. And what Jameson is describing here is the mortifying

cocoon of corporate structure – which deadens as it protects, which hollows out, absents, the manager, ensures that their attention is always displaced, ensures that they *cannot* listen. The delusion that many who enter into management with high hopes is precisely that they, the individual, can change things, that they will not repeat what *their* managers had done, that things will be different this time; but watch someone step up into management and it's usually not very long before the grey petrification of power starts to subsume them. It is here that structure is palpable – you can practically see it taking people over, hear its deadened/ deadening judgements speaking through them.

For this reason, it is a mistake to rush to impose the individual ethical responsibility that the corporate structure deflects. This is the temptation of the ethical which, as Žižek has argued, the capitalist system is using in order to protect itself in the wake of the credit crisis – the blame will be put on supposedly pathological individuals, those 'abusing the system', rather than on the system itself. But the evasion is actually a two step procedure – since structure *will* often be invoked (either implicitly or openly) precisely at the point when there is the possibility of individuals who belong to the corporate structure being punished. At this point, suddenly, the causes of abuse or atrocity are so systemic, so diffuse, that no individual can be held responsible. This was what happened with the Hillsborough football disaster, the Jean Charles De Menezes farce and so many other cases. But this impasse – it is only individuals that can be held ethically responsible for actions, and yet the cause of these abuses and errors is corporate, systemic – is not only a dissimulation: it precisely indicates what is lacking in capitalism. What agencies are capable of regulating and controlling impersonal structures? How is it possible to chastise a corporate structure? Yes, corporations can legally be treated as individuals – but the problem is that corporations, whilst certainly entities, are not like individual humans, and any analogy between punishing corporations and punishing individuals will therefore necessarily be poor. And it is not as if corporations are the deep-level agents behind everything; they are themselves constrained by/ expressions of the ultimate cause-that-is-not-a-subject: Capital.

9

Marxist Supernanny

Nothing could be a clearer illustration of what Žižek has identified as the failure of the Father function, the crisis of the paternal superego in late capitalism, than a typical edition of *Supernanny*. The program offers what amounts to a relentless, although of course implicit, attack on postmodernity's permissive hedonism. Supernanny is a Spinozist insofar as, like Spinoza, she takes it for granted that children are in a state of abjection. They are unable to recognize their own interests, unable to apprehend either the causes of their actions or their (usually deleterious) effects. But the problems that Supernanny confronts do not arise from the actions or character of the children – who can only be expected to be idiotic hedonists – but with the parents. It is the *parents'* following of the trajectory of the pleasure principle, the path of least resistance, that causes most of the misery in the families. In a pattern that quickly becomes familiar, the parents' pursuit of the easy life leads them to accede to their children's every demand, which become increasingly tyrannical.

Rather like many teachers or other workers in what used to be called 'public service', Supernanny has to sort out problems of socialization that the family can no longer resolve. A *Marxist* Supernanny would of course turn away from the troubleshooting of individual families to look at the structural causes which produce the same repeated effect.

The problem is that late capitalism insists and relies upon the very equation of desire with interests that parenting used to be based on rejecting. In a culture in which the 'paternal' concept of duty has been subsumed into the 'maternal' imperative to enjoy, it can seem that the parent is *failing* in their duty if they in any way impede their children's absolute right to enjoyment. Partly this is an effect of the increasing requirement that both parents work; in these conditions, when the parent sees the child very little, the tendency will often be to refuse to occupy the 'oppressive' function of telling the child what to do. The parental disavowal of this role is doubled at the level of cultural production by the refusal of 'gatekeepers' to do anything but give audiences what they already (appear to) want. The concrete question is: if a return to the paternal superego – the stern father in the home, Reithian superciliousness in broadcasting – is neither possible nor desirable, then how are we to move beyond the culture of monotonous moribund conformity that results from a refusal to challenge or educate? A question as massive as this cannot of course be finally answered in a short book such as this, and what follows here will amount to a few starting points and suggestions. In brief, though, I believe that it is Spinoza who offers the best resources for thinking through what a 'paternalism without the father' might look like.

In *Tarrying with the Negative*, Žižek famously argues that a certain Spinozism is the ideology of late capitalism. Žižek believes that Spinoza's rejection of deontology for an ethics based around the concept of health is allegedly flat with capitalism's amoral affective engineering. The famous example here is Spinoza's reading of the myth of the Fall and the foundation of Law. On Spinoza's account, God does not condemn Adam for eating the apple because the action is wrong; he tells him that he should not consume the apple because it will poison him. For Žižek, this dramatizes the termination of the Father function. An act is wrong not because Daddy says so; Daddy only says it is 'wrong' because performing the act will be harmful to us. In Žižek's view, Spinoza's move both deprives the grounding of Law in a sadistic act of scission (the cruel cut of castration), at the same time as it denies the ungrounded positing of agency in an act of pure volition, in which the subject assumes responsibility for everything. In fact, Spinoza has immense resources for analyzing the affective regime of late capitalism, the video-drome-control apparatus described by Burroughs, Philip K. Dick and David Cronenberg in which agency is dissolved in a phantasmagoric haze of psychic and physical intoxicants. Like Burroughs, Spinoza shows that, far from being an aberrant condition, addiction is the standard state for human beings, who are habitually enslaved into reactive and repetitive behaviors by frozen images (of themselves and the world). Freedom, Spinoza shows, is something that can be *achieved* only when we can apprehend the real causes of our actions, when we can set aside the 'sad passions' that intoxicate and entrance us.

There's no doubt that late capitalism certainly articulates many of its injunctions via an appeal to (a certain version of) health. The banning of smoking in public places, the relentless monstering of working class diet on programs like *You Are What You Eat*, do appear to indicate that we are already in the presence of a paternalism without the Father. It is not that smoking is 'wrong', it is that it will lead to our failing to lead long and enjoyable lives. But there are limits to this emphasis on good health: mental health and intellectual development barely feature at all, for instance. What we see instead is a reductive, hedonic model of health which is all about 'feeling and looking good'. To tell people how to lose weight, or how to decorate their house, is acceptable; but to call for any kind of cultural improvement is to be oppressive and elitist. The alleged elitism and oppression cannot consist in the notion that a third party might know someone's interest better than they know it themselves, since, presumably smokers are deemed either to be unaware of their interests or incapable of acting in accordance with them. No: the problem is that only certain types of interest are deemed relevant; since they reflect values that are held to be consensual. Losing weight, decorating your house and improving your appearance belong to the 'consentimental' regime.

In an excellent interview at the Register.com, the documentary film-maker Adam Curtis identifies the contours of this regime of affective management.

> TV now tells you what to feel.
>
> It doesn't tell you what to think any more. From EastEnders to reality format shows, you're on the emotional journey of people – and through the editing, it gently suggests to you what is the agreed form of feeling. "Hugs and Kisses", I call it.
>
> I nicked that off Mark Ravenhill who wrote a very good piece which said that if you analyse television now it's a system of guidance – it tells you who is having the Bad Feelings and who is having the Good Feelings. And the person who is having the Bad Feelings is redeemed through a "hugs and kisses" moment at the end. It really is a system not of moral guidance, but of emotional guidance.

Morality has been replaced by feeling. In the 'empire of the self' everyone 'feels the same' without ever escaping a condition of solipsism. 'What people suffer from,' Curtis claims,

> is being trapped within themselves – in a world of individualism everyone is trapped within their own feelings, trapped within their own imaginations. Our job as public service broadcasters is to take people beyond the limits of their own self, and until we do that we will carry on declining.
>
> The BBC should realize that. I have an idealistic view, but if the BBC could do that, taking people beyond their own selves, it will renew itself in a way that jumps over the competition. The competition is obsessed by serving people in their little selves. And in a way, actually, Murdoch for all

his power, is trapped by the self. That's his job, to feed the self.

In the BBC, it's the next step forward. It doesn't mean we go back to the 1950s and tell people how to dress, what we do is say "we can free you from yourself" – and people would love it.

Curtis attacks the internet because, in his view, it facilitates communities of solipsists, interpassive networks of like-minds who confirm, rather than challenge, each others' assumptions and prejudices. Instead of having to confront other points of view in a contested public space, these communities retreat into closed circuits. But, Curtis claims, the impact of internet lobbies on Old Media is disastrous, since, not only does its reactive pro-activity allow the media class to further abnegate its function to educate and lead, it also allows populist currents on both the left and the right to 'bully' media producers into turning out programming that is anodyne and mediocre.

Curtis's critique has a point, but it misses important dimensions of what is happening on the net. Contrary to Curtis's account of blogging, blogs can generate new discourse networks that have no correlate in the social field outside cyberspace. As Old Media increasingly becomes subsumed into PR and the consumer report replaces the critical essay, some zones of cyber-space offer resistance to a 'critical compression' that is elsewhere depressingly pervasive. Nevertheless, the interpassive simulation of participation in postmodern media, the network narcissism of MySpace and Facebook, has, in the main, generated content that is repetitive, parasitic and conformist. In a seeming irony, the media class's refusal to be paternalistic has not produced a bottom-up culture of breathtaking diversity, but one that is increasingly infantilized. By contrast, it is paternalistic cultures that treat audiences as adults, assuming that they can cope with cultural products that are complex and intellectually demanding. The reason that focus groups and capitalist feedback systems fail, even when they generate commodities that are immensely popular, is that people do not know what they want. This is not only because people's desire is already present but concealed from them (although this is often the case). Rather, the most powerful forms of desire are precisely cravings for the strange, the unexpected, the weird. These can only be supplied by artists and media professionals who are prepared to give people something different from that which already satisfies them; by those, that is to say, prepared to take a certain kind of risk. The Marxist Supernanny would not only be the one who laid down limitations, who acted in our own interests when we are incapable of recognizing them ourselves, but also the one prepared to take this kind of risk, to wager on the strange and our appetite for it. It is another irony that capitalism's 'society of risk' is much less likely to take this kind of risk than was the supposedly stodgy, centralized culture of the postwar social consensus. It was the public service-oriented BBC and Channel 4 that perplexed and delighted me with the likes of *Tinker, Tailor, Soldier Spy*, Pinter plays and Tarkovsky seasons; it was this BBC that also funded the popular avant gardism of the BBC Radiophonic Workshop, which embedded sonic experimentalism into everyday life. Such innovations are unthinkable now that the public has been displaced by the consumer. The effect of permanent structural instability, the 'cancellation of the long term', is invariably stagnation and conservatism, not innovation. This is not a paradox. As Adam Curtis's remarks above make clear, the affects that predominate in late capitalism are fear and cynicism. These emotions do not inspire bold thinking or entre-preneurial leaps, they breed conformity and the cult of the minimal variation, the turning out of products which very closely resemble those that are already successful. Meanwhile, films such as the aforementioned Tarkovsky's *Solaris* and *Stalker* – plundered by Hollywood since as far back as *Alien* and *Blade Runner* – were produced in the ostensibly moribund conditions of the Brezhnevite Soviet state, meaning that the USSR acted as a cultural entrepreneur for Hollywood. Since it is now clear that a certain amount of stability is necessary for cultural vibrancy, the question to be asked is: how can this stability be provided, and by what agencies?

It's well past time for the left to cease limiting its ambitions to the establishing of a big state. But being 'at a distance from the state' does not mean either abandoning the state or retreating into the private space of affects and diversity which Žižek rightly argues is the perfect complement to neoliberalism's domination of the state. It means recognizing that the goal of a genuinely new left should not be to take over the state but to subordinate the state to the general will. This involves, naturally, resuscitating the very concept of a general will, reviving – and modernizing – the idea of a public space that is not reducible to an aggregation of individuals and their interests. The 'methodological individualism' of the capitalist realist worldview presupposes the philosophy of Max Stirner as much as that of Adam Smith or Hayek in that it regards notions such as the public as 'spooks', phantom abstractions devoid of content. All that is real is the individual (and their families). The symptoms of the failures of this worldview are everywhere – in a disintegrated social sphere in which teenagers shooting each other has become commonplace, in which hospitals incubate aggressive superbugs – what is required is that effect be connected to structural cause. Against the postmodernist suspicion of grand narratives, we need to reassert that, far from being isolated, contingent problems, these are all the effects of a single systemic cause: Capital. We need to begin, as if for the first time, to develop strategies against a Capital which presents itself as ontologically, as well as geographically, ubiquitous.

Despite initial appearances (and hopes), capitalist realism was not undermined by the credit crisis of 2008. The speculations that capitalism might be on the verge of collapsing soon proved to be unfounded. It quickly became clear that, far from constituting the end of capitalism, the bank bail-outs were a massive re-assertion of the capitalist realist insistence that there is no alternative. Allowing the banking system to disintegrate was held to be *unthinkable*, and what ensued was a vast hemorrhaging of public money into private hands. Nevertheless, what did happen in 2008 was the collapse of the framework which has provided ideological cover for capitalist accumulation since the 1970s. After the bank bail-outs neoliberalism has, in every sense, been discredited. That is not to say that neoliberalism has disappeared overnight; on the contrary, its assumptions continue to dominate political economy, but they do so now no longer as part of an ideological project that has a confident forward momentum, but as inertial, undead defaults. We can now see that, while neoliberalism was necessarily capitalist realist, capitalist realism need not be neoliberal. In order to save itself, capitalism could revert to a model of social democracy or to a *Children of Men*-like authoritarianism. Without a credible and coherent alternative to capitalism, capitalist realism will continue to rule the political-economic unconscious.

But even if it is now evident that the credit crisis will not lead to the end of capitalism all by itself, the crisis has led to the relaxing of a certain kind of mental paralysis. We are now in a political landscape littered with what Alex Williams called 'ideological rubble' – it is year zero again, and a space has been cleared for a new anti-capitalism to emerge which is not necessarily tied to the old language or traditions. One of the left's vices is its endless rehearsal of historical debates, its tendency to keep going over Kronsdadt or the New Economic Policy rather than planning and organizing for a future that it really believes in. The failure of previous forms of anti-capitalist political organization should not be a cause for despair, but what needs to be left behind is a certain romantic attachment to the politics of failure, to the comfortable position of a defeated marginality. The credit crisis is an opportunity – but it needs to be treated as a tremendous speculative challenge, a spur for a renewal that is not a return. As Badiou has forcefully insisted, an effective anti-capitalism must be a rival to Capital, not a reaction to it; there can be no return to pre-capitalist territorialities. Anti-capitalism must oppose Capital's globalism with its own, authentic, universality.

It is crucial that a genuinely revitalized left confidently occupy the new political terrain I have (very provisionally) sketched here. Nothing is inherently political; politicization requires a political agent which can transform the taken-for-granted into the up-for-grabs. If neoliberalism triumphed by incorporating the desires of the post 68 working class, a new left could begin by building on the desires which neoliberalism has generated but which it has been unable to satisfy. For example, the left should argue that it can deliver what neoliberalism signally failed to do: a massive reduction of bureaucracy. What is needed is a new struggle over work and who controls it; an assertion of worker autonomy (as opposed to control by management) together with a rejection of certain kinds of labor (such as the excessive auditing which has become such a central feature of work in post-Fordism). This is a struggle that can be won – but only if a new political subject coalesces; it is an open question as to whether the old structures (such as the trade unions) will be capable of nurturing that subjectivity, or whether it will entail the formation of wholly new political organizations. New forms of industrial action need to be instituted against managerialism. For instance, in the case of teachers and lecturers, the tactic of strikes (or even of marking bans) should be abandoned, because they only hurt students and members (at the college where I used to work, one-day strikes were pretty much welcomed by management because they saved on the wage bill whilst causing negligible disruption to the college). What is needed is the strategic withdrawal of forms of labor which will only be noticed by management: all of the machineries of self-surveillance that have no effect whatsoever on the delivery of education, but which managerialism could not exist without. Instead of the gestural, spectacular politics around (noble) causes like Palestine, it's time that teaching unions got far more immanent, and take the opportunity opened up by the crisis to begin to rid public services of business ontology. When even businesses can't be run as businesses, why should public services?

We must convert widespread mental health problems from medicalized conditions into effective antagonisms. Affective disorders are forms of captured discontent; this disaffection can and must be channeled outwards, directed towards its real cause, Capital. Furthermore, the proliferation of certain kinds of mental illness in late capitalism makes the case for a new austerity, a case that is also made by the increasing urgency of dealing with environmental disaster. Nothing contradicts capitalism's constitutive imperative towards growth more than the concept of rationing goods and resources. Yet it is becoming uncomfortably clear that consumer self-regulation and the market will not by themselves avert environmental catastrophe. There is a libidinal, as well as a practical case, to be made for this new ascesis. If, as Oliver James, Žižek and *Supernanny* have shown, unlimited license leads to misery and disaffection, then limitations placed on desire are likely to quicken, rather than deaden, it. In any case, rationing of some sort is inevitable. The issue is whether it will be collectively managed, or whether it will be imposed by authoritarian means when it is already too late. Quite what forms this collective management should take is, again, an open question, one that can only be resolved practically and experimentally.

The long, dark night of the end of history has to be grasped as an enormous opportunity. The very oppressive pervasiveness of capitalist realism means that even glimmers of alternative political and economic possibilities can have a disproportionately great effect. The tiniest event can tear a hole in the grey curtain of reaction which has marked the horizons of possibility under capitalist realism. From a situation in which nothing can happen, suddenly anything is possible again.

Afterword

by Tariq Goddard

The atmosphere *Capitalist Realism* was written in was very much like the one the book describes, Mark alternating between the certainty that the finished work would be a portent of good things to come and an intermittent panic indistinguishable from gloom, based largely on the fear that he had written too little, too late. The journey the book underwent, from the drawing board to the final draft, proved to be longer than we had anticipated for a compact treatise. Two and a half years passed from my suggestion that Mark pen a work on belief, based on a blog post he wrote on *The Passion of Christ*, and his counter-suggestion that it be enlarged into a work of political theology, to his finishing the critique that rejected the prevailing socio-economic order he characterised as "Capitalist Realism".

There is always a lot invested in an author's first release, and to my surprise, Mark showed little interest in taking the pressure off himself. Unburdened by false modesty and assisted by messianic zeal, he confided that his book would be definitional for our new Zero series (on which point he was right) and that it was important for the new venture that he complete it quickly, adding that he felt he had a "big idea" book in him, and this might be it.

Having set the bar high, Mark then seemed a little daunted at its height, as it gradually became apparent that his was not the title we would launch the imprint with, and that the book as envisaged might not appear at all. The fundamental incongruence was that the material Mark had gradually assembled was at odds with a grand theoretical narrative, his notes resembling the observational vignettes and opinions on his *k-punk* blog, not a systemic work of theory. With the publication date looming and then delayed, we decided it was best to proceed with what he had, not with what Mark might yet write. What this was, when blended with his earlier notes, were personal reminiscences, reflections that might congeal round a set of blog posts on culture that he was looking to tweak and refine. That was not so unusual as the basis of a Zero book, but having promised so much, Mark was rather sheepish that the finished work would end up on the short side, claiming that while he still thought there was a good chance we could sell 1,000 copies (which was our holy grail at that time), the book would perhaps be the first of two parts, with a more "philosophical" section arriving at a future date.

When the manuscript was submitted, it was still in fragments, and the final draft had to be fashioned and assembled from its different parts rather than edited (or read) as a single chronological whole, further undermining the sense that this was in any way a conventional work of philosophy. As I too was already familiar with some of the material, if not its order, the impact the book would have on readers in its newly minted form was partly lost on both of us, and I admit to wondering whether some of Mark's readers might not feel slightly underwhelmed seeing relatively little new material. Mark certainly had a hard time making his mind up about it. Unlike some authors who cannot let go of their writing, he did not want to go back and fiddle with or change parts; rather, he just did not know whether the book was what he hoped it could be — nothing less than an attempt to understand the times we live in — or something less necessary, less illustrious.

The period up to publication was predictably fraught, and, in a manner reminiscent of politicians who move from nervous excitement bordering on triumphalism to an equally premature defeatism as the final tally of votes are counted, Mark's mood was subject to some extreme fluctuations. His initial apprehension was that the book would lack relevance. This was largely because he had not factored in or incorporated "the lessons" of the 2008 financial crash, speculating that the world's response to it might invalidate his thesis or render it a dated historical piece (which, sadly for the world but fortunately for his thesis, did not prove to be the case).[1] Moreover, although this was not the first time an author had mixed social observation with popular culture to diagnose a mood and coin a term, Mark was conscious of his role as an academic and media outsider, without the "qualifications" to be a societal seer, and he wondered whether critics would "get it". There was certainly scope for the book, like our entire series, to slip between genres and fall outside recognisable niches, especially as we did not even know how to classify it ourselves (settling on "philosophy" in lieu of anything better).

Though these reservations, at least as far as they related to *Capitalist Realism*, ultimately proved to be unfounded, they were not baseless. The reaction of Zero's then owner to the first few pages was apoplectic, raging that the book would not sell in the States because it cited an "obscure" British film (*Children of Men*) and that the tone was too "personal" to be popular, which initially, along with a cool response from buyers and the complete indifference of the media, seemed to bear out his objections. What few of us could have understood then was that the lack of love the book received from conventional quarters was, ironically, a harbinger of its future success. Despite the fact that many of our titles (to our surprise) were being very well reviewed in the mainstream press, *Capitalist Realism* was released to critical silence. To Mark's disbelief this would set a

---

1) The argument that capitalist realism was challenged if not usurped by the right, in particular the Trump and Johnson administrations, is one that Mark would have some sympathy with, as he believed that at some point the forces of political reaction would revert to "raw power" relations over obedience to the market.

lamentable trend that continued to his death. With the notable exception of a couple of music and film publications, none of his books was reviewed in print in his lifetime. Nor, with the exception of his incendiary mission statement found at the back of every Zero book (which ironically was misattributed to me by the panel on BBC2's *Late Review* programme, who ridiculed it for good measure while demolishing a novel of mine),[2] did any of his work feature on television or radio. With unfortunate timing Radio Four did have a plan for a walking tour of Felixstowe with Mark, but as this was mooted just a week before his death, it arrived too late ever to occur, or challenge his sense that he was uncelebrated or unrecognised outside our narrow milieu.

While it is common for many writers to feel like outsiders, not members of "the club", I think there was a genuinely discomfiting aspect to Mark and his work that set him at odds with the cultural commentariat of the day (his blistering attacks on them could not have helped), which explains why he was locked out of the citadel. But it was this very sense that he did not belong, that he had been passed over and would never count, expressed through his work (along with the un-shaming of the stigma surrounding madness and mental health), that inspired other outsiders who felt as invisible and unregarded as he did.

In the weeks after *Capitalist Realism*'s release, we watched steady sales grow exponentially until they were gathering speed out of any proportion to the publicity (or lack thereof) the book had enjoyed, the signal most longed for by publishers and writers alike — bona-fide, word-of-mouth success. A text that made little sense, or did not seem especially significant to journalists and academics, was picked up on and championed by

---

2) In a further irony this was a programme Mark watched, enjoyed, and had actually expressed a (never-to-be-fulfilled) desire to appear on the panel of, perhaps not recognising that his writing had already presented a perfectly viable alternative to "old" media of this sort.

literally thousands of readers in what seemed like a completely spontaneous response. Soon we were hearing from them at the events we organised and through the unsolicited feedback that had begun to stream in. It was heartening to learn that though many of them were students or in further education, as might be expected, many others were simply members of the reading public — in other words, the mainstream audience Mark had always wanted to reach. Furthermore, it was apparent that his book was not only touching individuals in private but also inspiring young people who were re-politicising en masse for the first time in nearly twenty years.

As the book continued to exceed our expectations and act as a flagship for the imprint (as it still does to this day), Mark's initial concerns gave way to the sense that the book was receiving no more than its due and, without any hubris or gloating that would have been alien to his character, that "publishing reality" had caught up with him ('In for a penny, in for a pound,' he laughed when news arrived that sales had first exceeded 10,000 copies). And that was pretty much how matters remained, until the last eight months of Mark's life when he began to express a certain ambivalence about the book's huge success.

I do not think it a coincidence that this occurred at the same time as a shift in his mood that would lead to his taking his own life. Increasingly he wondered aloud why the book should still be doing so well. This partly reflected his general loss of confidence in regard to himself and his writing, but also a genuine bafflement that a work he considered a steppingstone to the canonical book of theory he was struggling to write[3] should itself have become canonical. Why should *Capitalist Realism*'s sales be going from strength to strength while his projected "big" work remained elusive? It was a state of affairs Mark

---

3) At various times called *Communist Realism, Post Capitalist Desire* and *Acid Communism*.

struggled to make sense of, creating a cycle of self doubt and paralysis of which he was increasingly powerless to break out.

My reply to his misgivings was along the banal line that readers who had already bought the book kept finding more in it, and that its basic story of disappointment and hope would have a near-infinite resonance for newcomers, as long as the conditions he described resonated. With further hindsight, I would add that *Capitalist Realism*'s length and the "personal" vernacular in which it was written were also strengths; given a choice between Marx or Mark, the general reader would find that the latter speaks more directly to their daily lives.

Mark accepted my answer without being exactly satisfied by it, which was evinced by him returning to the question with a disturbing insistence. By then he may have well-known what we did not: The great system-building text was never going to be written, and his small book, *Capitalist Realism*, would be what we were left with in its place. Whether it is his most-accomplished work is irrelevant; it is his most-read. And for anyone who will progress no further in his oeuvre, there is the same pleasure to be had in reading it as there was in listening to Mark in person. Every line reflects the brilliant and episodic way in which Mark's mind worked in practice, seeing through comforting and discomforting fictions alike, and in doing so, is a more apt tribute to his intense and restless honesty than a formal work of philosophy could ever be. Mark may not have found consolation in that, but others still can, an irony he would have appreciated but not wished to dwell on. To do so would delay the moment when the grey curtain tears and 'suddenly anything is possible again', the utopian pact with his readers which his legacy is founded upon.

CULTURE, SOCIETY & POLITICS

Contemporary culture has eliminated the concept and public figure of the intellectual. A cretinous anti-intellectualism presides, cheer-led by hacks in the pay of multinational corporations who reassure their bored readers that there is no need to rouse themselves from their stupor. Zer0 Books knows that another kind of discourse - intellectual without being academic, popular without being populist - is not only possible: it is already flourishing. Zer0 is convinced that in the unthinking, blandly consensual culture in which we live, critical and engaged theoretical reflection is more important than ever before.

If you have enjoyed this book, why not tell other readers by posting a review on your preferred book site.

You may also wish to
subscribe to our Zer0 Books YouTube Channel.

Bestsellers from Zer0 Books include:

Poor but Sexy
Culture Clashes in Europe East and West
Agata Pyzik
How the East stayed East and the West stayed West.
Paperback: 978-1-78099-394-2 ebook: 978-1-78099-395-9

An Anthropology of Nothing in Particular
Martin Demant Frederiksen
A journey into the social lives of meaninglessness.
Paperback: 978-1-78535-699-5 ebook: 978-1-78535-700-8

In the Dust of This Planet
Horror of Philosophy vol. 1
Eugene Thacker
In the first of a series of three books on the Horror of
Philosophy,
In the Dust of This Planet offers the genre of horror as a way of
thinking about the unthinkable.
Paperback: 978-1-84694-676-9 ebook: 978-1-78099-010-1

The End of Oulipo?
An Attempt to Exhaust a Movement
Lauren Elkin, Veronica Esposito
Paperback: 978-1-78099-655-4 ebook: 978-1-78099-656-1

Capitalist Realism
Is There No Alternative?
Mark Fisher
An analysis of the ways in which capitalism has presented
itself as the only realistic political-economic system.
Paperback: 978-1-84694-317-1 ebook: 978-1-78099-734-6

Rebel Rebel
Chris O'Leary
David Bowie: every single song. Everything you want to know,
everything you didn't know.
Paperback: 978-1-78099-244-0 ebook: 978-1-78099-713-1

Cartographies of the Absolute
Alberto Toscano, Jeff Kinkle
An aesthetics of the economy for the twenty-first century.
Paperback: 978-1-78099-275-4 ebook: 978-1-78279-973-3

Malign Velocities
Accelerationism and Capitalism
Benjamin Noys
Long listed for the Bread and Roses Prize 2015, *Malign Velocities*
argues against the need for speed, tracking acceleration
as the symptom of the ongoing crises of capitalism.
Paperback: 978-1-78279-300-7 ebook: 978-1-78279-299-4

Babbling Corpse
Vaporwave and the Commodification of Ghosts
Grafton Tanner
Paperback: 978-1-78279-759-3 ebook: 978-1-78279-760-9

New Work New Culture
Work we want and a culture that strengthens us
Frithjof Bergmann
A serious alternative for mankind and the planet.
Paperback: 978-1-78904-064-7 ebook: 978-1-78904-065-4

Romeo and Juliet in Palestine
Teaching Under Occupation
Tom Sperlinger
Life in the West Bank, the nature of pedagogy and the role of a
university under occupation.
Paperback: 978-1-78279-637-4 ebook: 978-1-78279-636-7

Color, Facture, Art and Design
Iona Singh
This materialist definition of fine-art develops guidelines for
architecture, design, cultural-studies and ultimately social change.
Paperback: 978-1-78099-629-5 ebook: 978-1-78099-630-1

Sweetening the Pill
or How We Got Hooked on Hormonal Birth Control
Holly Grigg-Spall
Has contraception liberated or oppressed women? *Sweetening
the Pill* breaks the silence on the dark side of hormonal
contraception.
Paperback: 978-1-78099-607-3 ebook: 978-1-78099-608-0

Why Are We The Good Guys?
Reclaiming Your Mind from the Delusions of Propaganda
David Cromwell
A provocative challenge to the standard ideology that Western
power is a benevolent force in the world.
Paperback: 978-1-78099-365-2 ebook: 978-1-78099-366-9

The Writing on the Wall
On the Decomposition of Capitalism and its Critics
Anselm Jappe, Alastair Hemmens
A new approach to the meaning of social emancipation.
Paperback: 978-1-78535-581-3 ebook: 978-1-78535-582-0

Neglected or Misunderstood
The Radical Feminism of Shulamith Firestone
Victoria Margree
An interrogation of issues surrounding gender, biology,
sexuality, work and technology, and the ways in which our
imaginations continue to be in thrall to ideologies of maternity
and the nuclear family.
Paperback: 978-1-78535-539-4 ebook: 978-1-78535-540-0

How to Dismantle the NHS in 10 Easy Steps (Second Edition)
Youssef El-Gingihy
The story of how your NHS was sold off and why you will
have to buy private health insurance soon. A new expanded
second edition with chapters on junior doctors' strikes and
government blueprints for US-style healthcare.
Paperback: 978-1-78904-178-1 ebook: 978-1-78904-179-8

Digesting Recipes
The Art of Culinary Notation
Susannah Worth
A recipe is an instruction, the imperative tone of the expert,
but this constraint can offer its own kind of potential. A recipe
need not be a domestic trap but might instead offer escape –
something to fantasise about or aspire to.
Paperback: 978-1-78279-860-6 ebook: 978-1-78279-859-0

Most titles are published in paperback and as an ebook.
Paperbacks are available in traditional bookshops. Both print
and ebook formats are available online.
Follow us at: https://www.facebook.com/ZeroBooks
https://twitter.com/Zer0Books
https://www.instagram.com/zero.books